THE FASTING DAY

COOK BOOK

THE FASTING DAY COOKBOOK

120 EASY RECIPES FOR THE 5:2 DIET

PHOTOGRAPHY BY WILLIAM REAVELL

EBURY PRESS

3 5 7 9 10 8 6 4

Published in 2013 by Ebury Press, an imprint of Ebury Publishing

A Random House Group Company

The Random House Group Limited Reg. No. 954009

Addresses for companies within the Random House Group can be found at www.randomhouse.co.uk

A CIP catalogue record for this book is available from the British Library

The Random House Group Limited supports the Forest Stewardship Council® (FSC®), the leading international forest-certification organisation. Our books carrying the FSC label are printed on FSC®-certified paper. FSC is the only forest-certification scheme supported by the leading environmental organisations, including Greenpeace. Our paper procurement policy can be found at www.randomhouse.co.uk/environment

To buy books by your favourite authors and register for offers visit www.randomhouse.co.uk

Design by Seagull Design   Photography by William Reavell
Project editor: Laura Herring   Food stylist: Emma Marsden
Props stylist: Jo Harris   Consultant dietician: Fiona Hinton

Printed and bound in the UK by Butler Tanner and Dennis Ltd

ISBN 9780091955861

contents

introduction

There is much evidence associating low-calorie diets with many long-term health benefits. A restricted diet is thought to reduce our risk of developing serious illnesses like diabetes and cancer, and to help us live for longer. It is not altogether reasonable, however, to expect people to follow a continuously reduced-calorie diet, and more commonly it is recommended to include two low-calorie days each week, while the remainder of the time, eating normally. On fast days, women should consume no more than 500 calories, and men, no more than 600 calories.

During their fast days, many people choose to follow a traditional three-meals-a-day routine, with a low-calorie breakfast, lunch and dinner. Others prefer a light start to the day, saving up their calories for a hearty meal in the evening. Alternatively, you could start the day with a larger breakfast, eating just very small meals for the rest of the day. As long as you stay within your calories, you can mix-and-match in whatever way suits you best. *The Fasting Day Cookbook* allows you to do just this, with a delicious range of simple recipes for breakfast, lunch and dinner – and even a chapter on snacks and drinks – all of which you can eat, guilt-free, on your fasting days.

Each recipe includes a total calorie count at the top of the page and the calorie brackets are colour-coded for ease of use (see the table over the page) so that you can plan out your day – there are also some suggested meal plans on pages 180–7 covering a range of calorie limits.

Following a diet doesn't mean you have to miss out on all your favourite foods. In fact, flavour and variety are what will stop you feeling like you're on a diet at all. The recipes in this book make use of many slow-release energizers like oats, beans and lentils to help you feel fuller for longer, drawing inspiration from all kinds of cuisine, including Chinese, Indian, Thai and Italian. Start the day with a cranberry Morning Muffin (page 19), Huevos Rancheros (page 22) or a Low-cal Fry-up (page 32). Enjoy a midday meal of Grilled King Prawns with Chilli Soy Sauce (page 45) or Fattoush (page 53), and end your day with well-deserved Minted Lamb Escalopes (page 116), Chicken with Herby Nut Stuffing (page 127) or Lamb and Bamboo Shoot Red Curry (page 135). There is a wide variety to pick from, so you can eat different, exciting meals on every fast day.

For many dieters, snacking is a hard habit to break. *The Fasting Day Cookbook* has this covered too. With ideas from as low as 40 calories, choose from an irresistible range of snacks to see you through the day: Saffron Scones (page 159), Oaty Fruit Bites (page 160) or for when chocolate is the only answer, a luxurious Rich and Dark Spiced Hot Chocolate (page 163).

One of the main complaints when following a new eating plan is the amount of preparation involved, or the inconvenience of providing for other family members at mealtimes. Many of the recipes in *The Fasting Day Cookbook* are designed to serve four or more, meaning you can supplement them with extra side dishes to provide a filling meal for the rest of the family. Many other recipes are suitable for making in larger batches and freezing for upcoming diet days.

With such a tempting range of meals and snacks to choose from, you'll be able to eat just as well on your fast days as on your feast days!

Colour-coded calories
Using the easy-to-follow coloured stripes at the top of each recipe you can plan your daily intake at a glance. Each recipe also includes an exact calorie count.

○ 0–100 calories per serving

● 101–200 calories per serving

● 201–300 calories per serving

● 301–400 calories per serving

● 401–500 calories per serving

breakfast

Chilled Melon and Ginger Salad

CALORIES PER SERVING: 105

Serves 4 │ Preparation time: 15 minutes, plus chilling time │ Cooking time: 10 minutes

This simple summer salad features the winning combination of melon and ginger.
Here the mellow colours of several different melons blend together beautifully to
make a very pretty dish.

1 small charentais or
    cantaloupe melon
1 small galia melon
½ large honeydew
    melon
350g watermelon

for the dressing
2 tbsp caster sugar
1 tbsp chopped
    preserved stem
    ginger in syrup,
    drained
2 tbsp orange juice
2 tsp lemon juice

First make the dressing. Place the sugar and ginger in a
small saucepan with 120ml water. Heat gently to dissolve
the sugar, then bring to the boil and simmer for 10 minutes.

Transfer to a bowl and stir in the orange and lemon juices.
Set aside to cool.

Peel each melon and discard the seeds. Cut the flesh into
thin wedges and mix together in a large bowl.

Pour over the cooled dressing, stir well, cover and chill for
1 hour before serving.

Melon with Summer Fruits

CALORIES PER SERVING: 112

Serves 4 | Preparation time: 20 minutes, plus resting time

Cubes of scented, pale green and orange melon are tossed with red summer fruits in an orangey, melon sauce to make a delightful fruit salad. Choose melons that are very ripe. A ripe melon should give slightly when you apply pressure at the stem end.

½ galia melon
1 charentais melon
150ml freshly squeezed
    orange juice
125g strawberries
225g raspberries
4 tbsp fat-free Greek-
    style yoghurt
4 tsp clear honey

Cut the melons into thick wedges, then scoop out the seeds and remove the skin using a sharp knife. Cut the galia melon and half of the charentais melon into cubes and place in a serving bowl.

Roughly chop the remaining charentais melon and place in a blender with the orange juice. Process until smooth and then pour over the melon cubes.

Halve or quarter the strawberries, depending on their size, and add to the melon with the raspberries. Leave at room temperature for at least half an hour to allow the flavours to mingle before serving.

Serve with the Greek-style yoghurt and honey.

Mini Pancakes with Smoked Salmon

CALORIES PER SERVING: 136

Serves 2 | Preparation time: 10 minutes | Cooking time: 5 minutes

Smoked salmon always seems like such a treat. Served this way, it is filling and satisfying. The cool dressing, creamy salmon and hot pancakes make a luxurious breakfast.

2 tbsp quark
a squeeze of lemon
    juice
25g smoked salmon
2 tsp chopped chives
salt and pepper

for the pancakes
50g plain white flour
1 medium egg
2 tbsp semi-skimmed
    milk
4–6 sprays low-cal
    cooking spray
salt and white pepper

To make the pancakes, sift the flour into a bowl and season with the salt and white pepper. Make a well in the middle, crack in the egg and add the milk and 50ml water. Whisk the ingredients together briskly until combined.

Heat a non-stick frying pan over a medium heat and spray with the cooking spray. Place three large spoonfuls (half the mixture), well spaced apart, in the pan. Cook until bubbles appear on the surface and then flip the pancakes over and cook on the other side for a minute or two, until golden. Keep the pancakes warm under a piece of foil while you repeat with the rest of the batter.

Beat the quark with the lemon juice, and season to taste. Place three pancakes on each plate and top each with the quark mixture and the smoked salmon. Sprinkle with the chives.

Wholesome Porridge with Cinnamon

137

CALORIES PER SERVING: 137

Serves 1 | Preparation time: 5 minutes | Cooking time: 15 minutes

A traditional porridge breakfast has been given a delicious and healthy boost in this recipe. This warming dish will keep you going until lunch.

20g rolled oats
1 tsp mixed seeds, such as pumpkin, sunflower, sesame and poppy
8 sultanas
2 tbsp low-fat plain yoghurt
a pinch of cinnamon

Put the oats in a small pan. Add the seeds and sultanas and 130ml water. Bring to the boil and simmer for 5–10 minutes, until the water has been completely absorbed by the oats and the porridge is lovely and thick.

Spoon into a bowl, top with the yoghurt and sprinkle with the cinnamon.

Fruit and Yoghurt Parfait

164

CALORIES PER SERVING: 164

Serves 1 | Preparation time: 5 minutes | Cooking time: 2 minutes

A lovely, creamy and fruity start to the day. Use a combination of whatever fruits are in season and experiment with different varieties.

1 tbsp rolled oats
1 tsp golden caster sugar
¼ tsp mixed spice
1 tsp flaked almonds
100g fruit (use either chopped hard fruit or soft fruits)
100g low-fat plain yoghurt

Put the oats, sugar, mixed spice and almonds in a pan and heat for a couple of minutes until the flaked almonds have turned golden and the sugar has dissolved and starts to stick all the ingredients together.

Spoon half the fruit into a glass, top with half the yoghurt, then half the oat mixture. Repeat to make another layer, then serve.

Hinny Cakes with Blueberries

CALORIES PER SERVING: 168

Makes 10 | Preparation time: 10 minutes | Cooking time: 15–20 minutes

These lightly spiced cakes are pan-fried to give a soft, spongy texture on the inside and a sweet, crisp crust. Once fried, they're topped with fresh blueberries and lightly grilled to bring out the full scented flavour of the berries.

175g self-raising wholemeal flour
a pinch of salt
1 tsp baking powder
¼ tsp ground mace
¼ tsp ground cloves
75g unsalted butter
25g rice flour
25g caster sugar
90ml semi-skimmed milk
2 tbsp vegetable oil
225g blueberries
1 tbsp icing sugar

Sift the flour, salt, baking powder, mace and cloves into a bowl. Add 50g of the butter, cut into small pieces, and rub in using your fingertips until the mixture resembles fine breadcrumbs. Stir in the rice flour and caster sugar. Add the milk and mix until it forms a fairly soft dough, using a round-bladed knife.

Turn the dough out on to a lightly floured surface and knead very lightly. Cut into 10 even-sized pieces. Using lightly floured hands, shape each piece into a small flat cake.

Melt 15g of the remaining butter with half the oil in a large heavy-based frying pan or griddle. Place half of the cakes in the pan and fry gently over a medium-low heat for 3–4 minutes until golden underneath. Turn the cakes over and cook for a further 3–4 minutes until cooked through. Transfer to a large baking sheet. Melt the remaining butter with the oil and fry the rest of the cakes.

Preheat the grill to medium. Spoon the blueberries on to the cakes, piling them up slightly in the centre. Sprinkle with the sugar. Place under the grill for about 2 minutes, watching closely, until the blueberries are bubbling and the cake edges are lightly toasted. Serve immediately.

Note: It is essential to cook the cakes over a very gentle heat. A high temperature will overcook the crusts while the centres remain raw.

Morning Muffins

CALORIES PER SERVING: 175

Makes 12 | Preparation time: 15 minutes | Cooking time: 20 minutes

Moist muffins bursting with cranberries almost taste a little festive. Have all the dry ingredients mixed together, and prepare the muffin tin the night before. Serve straight from the oven – these muffins do not reheat well.

175g fresh cranberries
50g icing sugar, sifted
150g plain wholemeal
    flour
150g plain white flour
1 tbsp baking powder
1 tsp ground mixed
    spice
½ tsp salt
50g soft light brown
    sugar
1 medium egg
250ml semi-skimmed
    milk
60ml vegetable oil

Halve the cranberries and place in a bowl with the icing sugar. Toss gently to mix.

Line a 12-cup muffin tin with paper cases or simply grease with butter. Sift together the flours, baking powder, mixed spice, salt and brown sugar in a large bowl. Make a well in the centre.

Preheat the oven to 180°C/350°F/Mark 4. Beat the egg with the milk and oil. Add to the dry ingredients and stir just until blended, then lightly and quickly stir in the cranberries. The mixture should look roughly mixed, with lumps and floury pockets.

Fill the muffin cups two-thirds full with the mixture. Bake in the oven for about 20 minutes or until well risen and golden brown.

Transfer the muffins to a wire rack to cool slightly. Serve whilst still warm.

Honey and Yoghurt Muffins

180

CALORIES PER SERVING: 180

Makes 12 │ Preparation time: 15 minutes │ Cooking time: 20 minutes

These American-style muffins have a lovely subtle spice. They also freeze well.

225g plain white flour
1½ tsp baking powder
1 tsp bicarbonate of soda
a pinch of salt
½ tsp ground mixed spice
¼ tsp ground nutmeg
50g medium oatmeal,
   plus extra for dusting
50g light muscovado sugar
50g butter
225g Greek-style
   yoghurt
125ml milk
1 medium egg
4 tbsp clear honey

Preheat the oven to 200°C/400°F/Mark 6. Line a twelve-cup muffin tin with paper cases or simply grease with butter. Sift the flour, baking powder, bicarbonate of soda, salt, mixed spice and nutmeg into a bowl. Stir in the oatmeal and sugar.

Melt the butter and leave to cool slightly. Mix the yoghurt and milk together in a bowl, then beat in the egg, butter and honey. Pour over the dry ingredients and stir in quickly until just blended.

Divide the mixture equally between the muffin cups. Sprinkle with oatmeal and bake for about 20 minutes, until well risen and just firm to the touch. Remove from the oven and leave in the tins for 5 minutes, then transfer to a wire rack.

Breakfast Smoothie

190

CALORIES PER SERVING: 190

Serves 1 │ Preparation time: 5 minutes

Oats will help you stay fuller for longer and this rich and creamy smoothie tastes truly decadent. This is a fantastic way to begin your day with surprisingly few calories.

½ banana, chopped
2 tbsp rolled oats
75ml low-fat plain yoghurt
75ml skimmed milk
50g frozen berries

Put the banana pieces in a blender. Add the oats, yoghurt, milk and frozen fruits and whiz the mixture until smooth, then pour into a glass and serve.

Huevos Rancheros

CALORIES PER SERVING: 204

Serves 2 | Preparation time: 5 minutes | Cooking time: 20 minutes

This Mexican-inspired breakfast has a spicy kick to get your day started. You can serve this in one large dish or individual ramekins.

1 tsp olive oil
2 spring onions,
    chopped
½ red pepper, chopped
½ red chilli, finely
    chopped
1 x 200g tin of chopped
    tomatoes
1 tsp balsamic vinegar
2 medium eggs
1 wholemeal pitta bread
1 tbsp flat-leaf parsley
    or coriander, roughly
    chopped
salt and pepper

Heat the oil in a frying pan and fry the spring onions, red pepper and chilli for about 5 minutes, until softened and golden.

Add the chopped tomatoes and vinegar and season well. Bring to the boil and simmer for a couple of minutes, until thickened.

Make two wells in the middle of the pan and crack an egg into each. Cook until the whites have started to set, then cover and continue to cook until the white is completely cooked through.

Meanwhile, cut the pitta bread into triangles and toast lightly.

Divide the huevos rancheros between two plates and serve with a sprinkle of parsley or coriander and the toasted pitta.

Savoury Muffins

CALORIES PER SERVING: 215

Makes 6 | Preparation time: 15 minutes | Cooking time: 25–30 minutes

These may sound a bit strange for breakfast but they really hit the spot. These also freeze well; once cool, wrap in cling film and freeze for up to a month.

1 medium courgette, around 175g, grated

1 medium carrot, around 125g, grated

250g self-raising wholemeal flour

40g pecorino cheese, grated

a pinch of salt

½ tsp ground white pepper

175g low-fat plain yoghurt

50ml semi-skimmed milk

2 medium eggs

Preheat the oven to 200°C/400°F/Mark 6. Put the grated courgette and carrot in a large bowl. Add the flour, cheese, salt and pepper and toss roughly to mix everything together.

In a separate bowl, beat the yoghurt, milk and eggs. Make a well in the centre of the flour mixture and pour in the yoghurt mixture. Roughly combine all the ingredients together. Don't worry if there are still some floury patches, these will cook out once the muffins are baked.

Line a six-cup muffin tin with paper cases or simply grease with butter. Divide the mixture between the muffin cups and bake for 25–30 minutes, until a skewer pushed into the middle comes out clean.

Remove from the tin and cool on a wire rack until just warm, then serve.

Parma Ham, Melon and Ricotta Salad

CALORIES PER SERVING: 228

Serves 4 | Preparation time: 15 minutes, plus chilling time

Inspired by flavours now synonymous with Italian cuisine this is a particularly fresh-tasting salad that makes a surprisingly good breakfast.

150g ricotta cheese

2 tbsp chopped mixed
    fresh herbs, such as
    chervil, chives and
    basil

½ tsp lemon juice

1 small cantaloupe or
    charentais melon

125g Parma ham

12 black olives, stoned

50g watercress leaves

salt and pepper

finely pared lemon rind,
    shredded, to garnish

for the dressing

1 small ripe tomato

1 small shallot, peeled

1 small garlic clove,
    crushed

1 tsp grated lemon rind

1 tsp lemon juice

½ tbsp red wine vinegar

3 tbsp extra virgin olive oil

In a small bowl, beat the ricotta with the herbs, lemon juice and salt and pepper, to taste. Cover and chill for 30 minutes.

Meanwhile, prepare the dressing. Skin (see page 53), deseed and dice the tomato. Finely chop the shallot. Place all of the dressing ingredients in a small bowl and stir to combine. Season, to taste, with salt and pepper. Set aside until required.

Just before serving, cut the melon into wedges and scoop out the seeds. Peel and slice again into thin wedges.

Divide the melon slices between individual serving plates and top with the Parma ham, olives and watercress leaves. Top each salad with the ricotta.

Spoon over the dressing and garnish with lemon rind shreds.

Poached Egg, Florentine-style

CALORIES PER SERVING: 244

Serves 1 | Preparation time: 5 minutes | Cooking time: 20 minutes

A classic combination of eggs and spinach, minus the rich sauce. This has a great combination of flavours and will keep hunger at bay.

1 tsp butter

1 tomato, deseeded and
   diced

a large handful of
   spinach

1 medium egg

½ English muffin

1 tbsp freshly grated
   Parmesan cheese

salt and pepper

Heat the butter in a pan and add the tomato and spinach. Season well with salt and pepper. Cook for a couple of minutes, until the spinach has just wilted.

Bring a small pan of water to the boil. Stir the water with a spoon to create a swirl, then crack the egg into a small bowl and slide the egg into the middle of the swirl. Poach for 3–4 minutes until the white is firm and opaque.

Toast the muffin and place on a plate. Spoon the spinach and tomato mixture on top. Using a slotted spoon, lift the poached egg out of the water and drain on kitchen paper. Place on top of the spinach mixture and sprinkle with the Parmesan. Season well and serve.

Eggs with Smoked Salmon

CALORIES PER SERVING: 249

Serves 4 | Preparation time: 5 minutes | Cooking time: 3–5 minutes

This can be made in the time it takes to boil an egg. It's best if the crème fraîche is at room temperature when you use it.

4 medium eggs
100g smoked salmon
50ml crème fraîche
1 tsp black peppercorns
4 slices of wholemeal
    toast, each spread
    with 1 tsp butter
chopped chives or
    mustard cress,
    to garnish

Lower the eggs into a pan of simmering water, making sure that the water covers them completely. Cook for 3½–5 minutes until soft-boiled. Drain and rinse under cold running water until they are cool enough to handle, then shell them.

While the eggs are cooking, chop the smoked salmon roughly and mix into the crème fraîche. Crack the black peppercorns, using a pestle and mortar.

Halve the eggs and arrange on individual serving plates. Trickle the smoked salmon sauce over them. Scatter on the cracked black peppercorns and garnish with chives or mustard cress. Serve at once with hot toast.

Low-cal Fry-up

CALORIES PER SERVING: 276 with toast; 167 without toast

Serves 1 │ Preparation time: 5 minutes │ Cooking time: 10 minutes

Counting the calories, doesn't mean you have to miss out on all the fun! With a few tweaks you can enjoy all your favourites.

4 sprays low-cal
　　cooking spray
1 rasher back bacon,
　　trimmed of fat
4 cherry tomatoes,
　　halved
2 large chestnut
　　mushrooms or
　　4 baby chestnut
　　mushrooms,
　　quartered or halved
1 medium egg
salt and pepper
optional: 1 slice of
　　wholemeal toast,
　　spread with 1 tsp
　　butter

Spray a large frying pan with the cooking spray and add the bacon, tomatoes and mushrooms. Cook over a medium heat for 5 minutes, until softened. Season well with salt and pepper.

Spoon the mushrooms, tomatoes and bacon to the side and crack the egg into the middle of the pan. Cook over a medium heat for a couple of minutes and then cover with a lid and continue to cook until the egg white is completely set. Check the seasoning and then serve with a slice of hot buttered toast, if liked.

Spiced Winter Fruit Compote

CALORIES PER SERVING: 290

Serves 2 | Preparation time: 10 minutes, plus cooling time | Cooking time: 50 minutes

Dried fruits are poached in apple juice and sumptuously scented with star anise and cinnamon. Served with thick Greek-style yoghurt, this is an exotic way to begin your low-calorie day.

50g ready-to-eat dried pears

50g ready-to-eat dried figs

50g ready-to-eat dried apricots

50g ready-to-eat prunes

100ml apple juice

1 star anise

½ cinnamon stick

2 tsp light muscovado sugar

110ml Greek-style yoghurt

a pinch of ground cinnamon

Put the fruit in a saucepan with the apple juice, star anise and cinnamon stick. Place over a low heat and bring slowly to the boil.

Reduce the heat, cover the pan and simmer for 45 minutes until the fruits are plump and tender. Check the liquid during cooking to ensure there is sufficient; add a little water if necessary.

Scrape the compote into a bowl. Taste for sweetness, and add a little sugar if necessary. Allow to cool to room temperature.

To serve, divide the compote between individual glass dishes. Top with yoghurt and a light sprinkling of cinnamon.

Bircher Muesli

CALORIES PER SERVING: 317

Serves 1 │ Preparation time: 5 minutes, plus resting time │ Cooking time: 2 minutes

Deliciously moist oats with fresh apple and chopped dried figs rounded off with creamy yoghurt. Make this the day before so the flavours have a chance to mingle.

3 tbsp rolled oats
1 ready-to-eat dried fig,
    finely chopped
½ apple, grated
90ml semi-skimmed
    milk
50ml low-fat plain
    yoghurt
3 tsp flaked almonds
a pinch of ground
    cinnamon

Put the oats, chopped fig, apple, milk and yoghurt in a bowl and mix together well. Chill in the fridge for a minimum of 30 minutes or overnight.

When ready to serve, toast the flaked almonds in a dry frying pan until just golden. Spoon the muesli into a bowl, top with the almonds and sprinkle with cinnamon.

Roasted Peaches with Pistachio Stuffing

CALORIES PER SERVING: 350

Serves 2 | Preparation time: 15 minutes | Cooking time: 20 minutes

Flavourful fresh peaches are stuffed with a lightly spiced crunchy filling of amaretti biscuit crumbs and pale green pistachios, then baked until slightly soft. Choose peaches that are almost, but not quite, ripe enough to eat.

50g amaretti biscuits

75g shelled pistachio nuts

25g light muscovado sugar

¼ tsp Chinese five spice

2 medium egg yolks

6 peaches

4 tbsp Greek-style yoghurt or crème fraîche

Preheat the oven to 180°C/350°F/Mark 4. Roughly crush the amaretti biscuits between two sheets of greaseproof paper, using a rolling pin; or by processing briefly in a food processor. Finely chop the pistachios. Mix the crushed biscuits and pistachios in a bowl with the sugar, spice and egg yolks.

Cut the peaches in half and remove the stones. Pile the nut filling into the peach halves and place them in a baking dish. Pour 150ml water around the peaches and bake in the oven for 20 minutes or until the peaches are soft.

Transfer the stuffed peaches to individual serving plates and serve immediately, accompanied by the yoghurt or crème fraîche.

Grilled Herrings with Oatmeal, Spinach and Almonds

CALORIES PER SERVING: 374

Serves 4 | Preparation time: 15 minutes | Cooking time: 15 minutes

Herrings are perfect for grilling, their oily, silvery skins turning beautifully crisp, charred and appetizing. These herrings have a moist, tumbling spinach, almond and oatmeal stuffing, held together with a little melting Cheddar.

4 herrings, boned
2 tsp balsamic or wine
   vinegar

for the stuffing
25g butter
1 onion, peeled and
   finely chopped
25g blanched almonds,
   chopped
125g young spinach
   leaves, tough stalks
   removed
25g medium oatmeal
50g mature Cheddar
   cheese, grated
salt and pepper
lemon wedges, to serve

To make the stuffing, melt the butter in a frying pan. Add the onion and almonds and fry for 3 minutes. Stir in the spinach and cook until just wilted.

Remove from the heat and stir in the oatmeal. Cool slightly, then add the cheese and a little seasoning.

Score the herrings, several times on each side. Sprinkle the vinegar inside the cavities and over the skins.

Spoon the prepared stuffing into the cavities and secure the opening with wooden cocktail sticks.

Preheat the grill to medium. Lightly oil a sheet of foil and use it to line a grill pan (this will stop the fish from sticking to the pan and also make it easier to clear up any filling that escapes during cooking). Place the herrings in the pan and grill for 15 minutes, turning over, halfway through cooking.

Transfer the herrings to warmed serving plates and serve with lemon wedges.

Asparagus with Poached Eggs

CALORIES PER SERVING: 400

Serves 6 | Preparation time: 20 minutes | Cooking time: 40 minutes

Fresh asparagus in season is not to be missed. This is such a classic pairing and the potatoes make it a filling start to the day.

900g asparagus
700g small new
   potatoes, scrubbed
300ml crème fraîche
   or whipped double
   cream
3 tbsp tarragon vinegar
3 tbsp chopped
   tarragon, plus extra
   to garnish
6 medium eggs,
   refrigerated
salt and pepper

Peel the tough skin from the lower end of the asparagus stalks and then trim the stalks to an even length.

Fill a roasting tin with cold water and add a little salt. Bring to the boil and lay the asparagus in the tin. Boil for 10–15 minutes or longer, depending on the variety and thickness of the stalks.

Lift the asparagus out of the roasting tin and immediately plunge into a bowl of cold water to set the colour and stop the cooking. Set aside.

Pour the asparagus water into a saucepan, add the potatoes and cook for 15–20, minutes until tender. Using a slotted spoon, transfer the potatoes to a colander and cool slightly. Reserve the water for poaching the eggs.

Mix the crème fraîche with 1 tablespoon of the vinegar. Stir in the tarragon, season, cover and refrigerate.

Slice the potatoes and arrange on serving plates. Season well. Drain and dry the asparagus on kitchen paper and lay over the potatoes.

Bring the reserved asparagus water to a rolling boil in a large shallow pan, adding the remaining 2 tablespoons of vinegar and more water if necessary. Break the eggs into the bubbling water, then turn down to a bare simmer. Poach for 3–4 minutes – ideally they should still be quite soft. Lift out carefully, drain on kitchen paper and arrange on the asparagus. Season and serve at once, with the tarragon cream and garnished with extra tarragon.

lunch

Mushroom Pâté with Madeira

CALORIES PER SERVING: 100

Serves 6 │ Preparation time: 15 minutes, plus soaking time │ Cooking time: 20–25 minutes

You can use any combination of mushrooms in this rich pâté, but try to include some flavourful wild ones or cultivated dark field mushrooms. Don't be tempted to use all button mushrooms, as the end result will lack colour and flavour.

15g dried porcini mushrooms
150ml semi-skimmed milk
1 small onion
1 garlic clove
25g butter
350g mushrooms
125g ricotta cheese
1 tbsp Madeira
½ tsp balsamic vinegar or lemon juice
1 tsp mushroom ketchup
freshly grated nutmeg, to taste
1–2 tbsp chopped flat-leaf parsley or coriander, plus extra to garnish
coarse sea salt and pepper

Rinse the porcini under cold running water to wash away the grit, then place in a bowl. Pour on the warm milk and leave to soak for 20 minutes. Drain the porcini and chop finely.

Peel and finely chop the onion and garlic. Melt the butter in a saucepan, add the onion and garlic and fry gently for 5–10 minutes until softened and transparent.

Meanwhile, wipe the fresh mushrooms with a damp cloth to clean them, then chop finely.

Add the porcini and fresh mushrooms to the onion and garlic, increase the heat a little and cook, stirring occasionally, for about 15 minutes until the mushrooms are tender and reduced to a thick pulp. Leave to cool slightly.

Transfer the mushroom mixture to a food processor or bowl. Add the ricotta, Madeira, balsamic vinegar, mushroom ketchup and nutmeg and process very briefly or stir until evenly mixed; the pâté should have a coarse texture. Stir in the chopped parsley or coriander and adjust the seasoning.

Turn into a serving dish or individual ramekins and garnish with parsley or coriander.

Spicy Grilled Aubergine Salad

CALORIES PER SERVING: 100

Serves 4 | Preparation time: 25 minutes, plus resting time | Cooking time: 10 minutes

For this unusual salad, baby aubergine slices are brushed with a sweet soy glaze, then grilled until charred and tender and tossed with green beans in a sesame and lime dressing. Serve the salad while it is still warm.

4 baby aubergines
2 tsp sea salt
2 tbsp sweet soy sauce
2 tsp Thai fish sauce
1 tsp hot chilli sauce
1 tsp lemon juice
½ tsp ground cumin
½ tsp clear honey
125g green beans

for the dressing
1 tbsp groundnut or
    sunflower oil
1 tsp sesame oil
1 tbsp lime juice
a pinch of sugar

to serve
½ lettuce
2 tbsp lime juice
sesame seeds
mint leaves

Trim the aubergines and cut each one into 4 slices. Place the aubergines in a colander set over a plate and sprinkle over the salt. Leave for 30 minutes so the aubergines can release their bitter juices.

Meanwhile, in a small bowl mix together the sweet soy sauce, fish sauce, chilli sauce, lemon juice, cumin and honey. Set aside.

Top and tail the beans and cut into 5cm lengths. Bring a large pan of lightly salted water to a rolling boil, plunge in the green beans, return to the boil and cook for 3 minutes until the beans are tender. Immediately drain and refresh the beans under cold running water. Drain again.

Preheat the grill to high. Rinse the aubergines to remove the salt and pat dry. Place on a rack over the grill pan and brush with half the soy sauce mixture. Grill as close to the heat as possible for 2–3 minutes. Turn the slices over, brush with the remaining soy mixture and grill until charred and tender.

Whisk the ingredients for the dressing together until evenly blended. Toss the green beans with half of the dressing.

Tear the lettuce into bite-sized pieces, toss with the lime juice and arrange on individual serving plates. Top with the aubergine slices and beans, then drizzle over the remaining dressing. Scatter over some sesame seeds and mint leaves and serve at once.

Sugar Snap Peas with a Minted Lemon Dip

CALORIES PER SERVING: 105

Serves 4 | Preparation time: 10 minutes | Cooking time: 5–10 minutes

Sugar snap peas are available all year round. In this low-calorie lunch they are served with a light crème fraîche dipping sauce, flavoured with fresh mint and lemon.

450g sugar snap peas

for the sauce
4 tbsp crème fraîche
1 tbsp finely shredded
    or chopped mint
finely pared or grated
    zest and juice of
    ½ lemon
90ml Greek-style
    yoghurt
coarse sea salt and
    pepper

Top and tail the sugar snap peas, then steam or cook them in boiling water until just tender.

Prepare the sauce: put all the ingredients in a bowl, reserving a little lemon zest to garnish. Stir together and season with salt and pepper, to taste.

Drain the sugar snap peas and spoon the yoghurt sauce into a small serving dish. Garnish with the reserved lemon zest and serve at once.

Spicy Beef Soup

CALORIES PER SERVING: 115

Serves 4 | Preparation time: 30 minutes | Cooking time: 15 minutes

A comforting and surprisingly filling soup with lots of flavour – add a few chilli flakes for even more heat. Make sure you use lean pieces of beef; minute steak is perfect for this dish.

1.2 litres vegetable stock

1 red chilli, deseeded and diced

1 tbsp Thai fish sauce

2 tbsp rice vinegar

1 tbsp chilli sauce

100g baby chestnut mushrooms, finely sliced

1 red pepper, finely sliced

100g baby corn, finely sliced

1 small carrot, finely sliced

200g lean beef, cut into strips

1 tsp chilli oil

2 tbsp coriander leaves

Put the vegetable stock into a pan and add the chilli, fish sauce, vinegar and chilli sauce. Bring to the boil and simmer gently for 10 minutes.

Add the mushrooms, pepper, corn and carrot, and simmer for a further 10 minutes.

Stir in the beef strips and continue to simmer, until cooked to your liking. Ladle into four bowls and serve with a dash of chilli oil and the coriander leaves.

Grilled King Prawns with Chilli Soy Sauce

CALORIES PER SERVING: 120

Serves 4 | Preparation time: 20 minutes, plus marinating | Cooking time: 20 minutes

This is a dish that definitely requires a finger bowl! It's a messy business, but what could be better than dipping succulent grilled prawns into a rich, tangy dip?

12 large raw tiger
    prawns, shelled
1 tbsp chopped
    coriander
lime wedges, to serve

for the marinade
1 garlic clove, peeled
1 red chilli, deseeded
1 tbsp sesame oil
2 tbsp dark soy sauce
grated zest and juice of
    2 limes
1 tbsp soft brown sugar

for the chilli soy sauce
1 tsp crushed chilli
    flakes
1 tbsp lime juice
2 tbsp dark soy sauce
1 tbsp Thai fish sauce
2 tbsp soft brown sugar

To prepare the prawns, use a sharp knife to slit each one down the back and remove the black intestinal vein. Rinse in cold water and dry on kitchen paper, then place in a shallow non-reactive dish. To make the marinade, finely chop the garlic and chilli and mix with the remaining ingredients. Pour over the prawns and stir well to coat. Cover the dish and leave to marinate in a cool place for at least 4 hours, preferably overnight.

For the chilli soy sauce, place all the ingredients in a small pan with 2 tablespoons of cold water and bring to the boil, stirring until the sugar is dissolved. Remove the pan from the heat and leave to cool.

Just before serving, preheat the grill to medium. Transfer the prawns to the grill pan and grill as close to the heat as possible for 6–8 minutes, turning and basting frequently with the marinade juices, until the prawns are pink and lightly charred.

Transfer the prawns to a warmed serving platter and scatter over the chopped coriander. Serve with lime wedges and the chilli sauce for dipping. Don't forget the finger bowls!

Tuscan Bean Soup with Toasted Garlic

CALORIES PER SERVING: 159

Serves 6 | Preparation time: 20 minutes, plus soaking time | Cooking time: 1 hour 10 minutes

A substantial white bean soup. If the soup is thicker than you like, thin it down with a little extra water or stock. This makes a lot of soup, but it's excellent to freeze – reheat it straight from frozen.

225g dried white haricot or cannellini beans
4 garlic cloves, peeled
50ml olive oil
1–2 tbsp chopped flat-leaf parsley
salt and pepper

Put the dried beans in a bowl and pour on enough cold water to cover. Leave to soak overnight.

The next day, preheat the oven to 170°C/325°F/Mark 3. Drain the beans and place in a flameproof casserole. Cover with cold water to 5cm above the beans. Bring to the boil, then cover tightly and bake in the oven for about 1 hour or until tender (see note). Keep them in their cooking liquid.

Meanwhile, finely chop half the garlic and thinly slice the remainder.

Transfer half of the beans and liquid to a food processor or blender and process until smooth. Add this purée to the beans in the casserole and stir well.

Heat half the olive oil in a frying pan, add the chopped garlic and fry gently until soft and golden. Stir into the soup and reheat until boiling. Simmer gently for 10 minutes. Taste and season well with salt and pepper. Pour into a warmed tureen or individual soup bowls.

Heat the remaining olive oil in the frying pan and fry the sliced garlic until golden. Spoon over the soup and serve at once, sprinkled with the chopped parsley.

Note: The cooking time depends on the freshness of the beans. Older beans will take longer to cook. Begin testing them after 45 minutes.

Chilled Beetroot and Apple Soup

CALORIES PER SERVING: 160

Serves 4 │ Preparation time: 10 minutes

A cool, deep crimson soup that's as wonderfully refreshing to eat as it looks. Serve it topped with a dollop of the minted cucumber cream.

350g cooked, peeled beetroot
juice of ½ lemon
600ml unsweetened apple juice, chilled
200g Greek-style yoghurt, chilled
cayenne pepper, to taste
10cm piece cucumber
6 mint leaves, finely chopped
salt and pepper
8 chives, to garnish

Slice the beetroot and place in a food processor or blender. Add the lemon juice, half the apple juice and half the yoghurt. Process for a couple of minutes until smooth.

Pour the beetroot mixture into a mixing bowl, stir in the rest of the apple juice and season, to taste, with salt, pepper and cayenne pepper. Chill until you are ready to serve, then pour into individual bowls.

To make the cucumber cream, grate the cucumber and stir into the remaining yoghurt. Stir the mint into the mixture. Spoon some cucumber cream into the middle of each serving and sprinkle with a little cayenne pepper. Snip the chives over the top to garnish.

Prawn and Rice Noodle Salad

CALORIES PER SERVING: 171

Serves 4 | Preparation time: 15 minutes | Cooking time: 1 minute

This is a very pretty Thai-style salad, packed with flavour. The dressing is deliciously sharp and sweet and the rice noodles are pleasingly low in calories.

50g dried rice noodles
75g shiitake mushrooms
1 large carrot
1 large courgette
175g large cooked
    prawns, shelled
1 tbsp toasted sesame
    seeds
2 tbsp chopped
    coriander

for the dressing
2 garlic cloves
1 tbsp light soy sauce
2 tbsp sugar
1 tbsp wine vinegar
1 tbsp sesame oil
1 red chilli

First make the dressing. Crush the garlic and mix with the soy sauce, sugar, wine vinegar and sesame oil in a small bowl. Cut the chilli in half lengthwise, remove the seeds, then cut into very fine strips. Mix into the dressing.

Cut the noodles into 10cm lengths. Cook in boiling water according to the packet instructions. Drain thoroughly and refresh under cold running water. Drain again.

Trim the mushrooms and slice finely. Add to the dressing and mix thoroughly.

Cut the carrot and courgette into fine julienne, or matchstick strips.

Place the noodles in a bowl and add the mushrooms with the dressing, the carrot and courgette, and the prawns. Toss the salad well to combine all the ingredients. Sprinkle with the sesame seeds and chopped coriander to serve.

Chickpeas with Ginger and Tomato

CALORIES PER SERVING: 175

Serves 6 | Preparation time: 5 minutes, plus overnight soaking | Cooking time: 2 hours

The flavour in this dish is improved if it is made the day before required and reheated. If you don't have the time for soaking and cooking dried chickpeas, use tinned ones instead – they work equally well (see note).

225g dried chickpeas
5cm piece fresh root
    ginger
2 garlic cloves
1 tbsp olive oil
2 tsp garam masala
1 x 400g tin of chopped
    tomatoes
2 spring onions
150ml Greek-style
    yoghurt
1 tsp mild curry paste
2 tbsp chopped mint
2 tbsp chopped
    coriander
salt and pepper
coriander and mint
    sprigs, to garnish

Put the chickpeas in a large bowl and pour on enough cold water to cover. Leave to soak overnight.

The next day, drain the chickpeas and put them in a large saucepan with enough fresh cold water to cover. Bring to the boil and boil steadily for 10 minutes, then lower the heat and simmer for about 1½ hours, until the chickpeas are really tender, adding salt towards the end of the cooking time. Drain thoroughly.

Peel and finely chop the ginger and garlic. Heat the oil in the saucepan and add the ginger, garlic and garam masala. Sauté for 2 minutes, then add the tomatoes and chickpeas and bring to the boil. Reduce the heat and simmer gently for 15 minutes.

Meanwhile, trim and finely chop the spring onions. Place in a bowl with the yoghurt, curry paste, mint and coriander. Mix thoroughly and season liberally with salt and pepper.

Turn the chickpeas into a serving bowl and swirl in the yoghurt mixture. Serve immediately, garnished with coriander and mint sprigs.

Note: Replace the dried chickpeas with two 400g tins of chickpeas. Drain and rinse thoroughly under cold running water and add with the tomatoes as above.

Fattoush

CALORIES PER SERVING: 180

Serves 4 | Preparation time: 15 minutes | Cooking time: 3 minutes

A gloriously flavourful Arabic salad that's reminiscent of a solid gazpacho. This makes a wonderfully filling lunch and is easy to transport in a lunchbox.

4 tomatoes
½ cucumber
4 spring onions
1 small green pepper
1 garlic clove, crushed
juice of ½ lemon
2 tbsp finely chopped
    flat-leaf parsley
2 tbsp roughly torn
    mint leaves
3 tbsp olive oil
1 wholemeal pitta bread
12 black olives, stoned
    and chopped
salt and pepper

Preheat the grill to medium. Put the tomatoes into a heatproof bowl and pour on boiling water to cover. Leave for 1 minute, then drain and remove the skins. Cut them up roughly and place in a food processor or blender. Cut the cucumber roughly and place in the food processor too.

Trim and roughly chop the spring onions. Halve, core and deseed the green pepper, then roughly chop the flesh. Add the spring onions and green pepper to the food processor with the garlic and lemon juice. Process to a chunky purée.

Turn the mixture into a bowl and stir in the chopped parsley, mint, olive oil, salt and pepper.

Toast the pitta bread briefly on both sides. Break into small pieces and scatter over the salad.

Transfer the salad to a serving dish and stud with black olives.

Note: You can make this salad by hand if you prefer, chopping all the vegetables finely, but it will take a little longer.

Fennel and Orange Salad

CALORIES PER SERVING: 185

Serves 4 | Preparation time: 15 minutes

Fennel with orange is a fairly classic combination, though here it is enhanced with a rich olive pesto, which works particularly well with the orange. Blood oranges are the ideal choice when in season, as they have a delicious sweet flavour and pretty ruby-coloured flesh.

2 large oranges
1 medium fennel bulb
1 small red onion
50g rocket leaves

for the dressing
15g pitted black olives
1 sun-dried tomato in
    oil, drained
1 small garlic clove,
    crushed
½ tbsp chopped flat-
    leaf parsley
4 tbsp extra virgin olive oil
2 tsp balsamic vinegar
salt and pepper

First make the dressing. Roughly chop the olives and sun-dried tomato. Place in a blender or food processor with the garlic, parsley and 1 tablespoon of oil. Blend to form a fairly smooth paste. Transfer to a bowl and whisk in the remaining oil, vinegar and seasoning to taste.

Peel the oranges, removing all the white pith, then cut into segments between the membranes and place in a large bowl.

Discard the tough outer layer from the fennel, then slice very thinly. Finely slice the onion.

Add the fennel, onion and rocket to the oranges. Pour over the dressing and toss well until evenly coated. Serve at once.

Spicy Parsnip and Carrot Soup with Cumin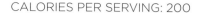

CALORIES PER SERVING: 200

Serves 4 | Preparation time: 15 minutes | Cooking time: 15–20 minutes

A warming vegetarian soup, with a delicious hint of spicy cumin seeds. As the parsnip and carrot purée is sufficient to thicken the soup, there are no added calories in the form of flour. For optimum flavour, use home-made vegetable stock.

450g parsnips

225g carrots

2 tbsp olive oil

1 onion, peeled and
    finely chopped

1 tbsp curry powder

350ml vegetable stock

300ml semi-skimmed
    milk

salt and pepper

2 tsp cumin seeds,
    to garnish

Peel the parsnips, cut in half and remove the woody stems. Peel the carrots. Cut the parsnips and carrots into even-sized pieces.

Heat the oil in a heavy-based saucepan, add the vegetables, including the onion, and stir to lightly coat in the oil. Cover and cook for a few minutes until the vegetables are slightly softened. Sprinkle in the curry powder and cook, stirring, for 1 minute.

Stir in the vegetable stock and milk, and season with salt and pepper. Bring to the boil, then reduce the heat to a gentle simmer and cook for 15–20 minutes until the vegetables are soft.

Allow the soup to cool a little, then transfer to a blender or food processor and work until smooth. If the consistency is a little too thick for your liking, add a splash of vegetable stock.

Toast the cumin seeds by gently frying them in a non-stick pan, or spread on a baking sheet and grill under a medium heat. Meanwhile, return the soup to the saucepan and reheat gently. Serve the soup in warmed soup bowls, garnished with a sprinkling of cumin seeds.

French Bean and Omelette Ribbon Salad

CALORIES PER SERVING: 210

Serves 4 | Preparation time: 15 minutes | Cooking time: 10 minutes

Thin strips of omelette festoon slim French beans in this pretty salad, which is enhanced by a vigorous dressing full of Mediterranean flavours.

2 medium eggs
50ml olive oil
350g French beans
1 large garlic clove
1 tsp red wine vinegar
1 tsp balsamic vinegar
2 sun-dried tomatoes,
    in oil, drained
1 tsp capers
salt and pepper

Break the eggs into a bowl, season with salt and pepper and beat lightly with a fork. Smear an 18–20cm frying pan (preferably non-stick) with a little olive oil and place over a medium heat. When it is hot, pour in half the egg mixture and swirl the pan to spread the mixture quickly. It will set almost immediately into a thin omelette. Turn out on to a plate and repeat with the remaining egg, turning it out on to a separate plate.

Top and tail the French beans and cook them in a little boiling salted water for about 5 minutes. Drain and spread in a serving dish.

Peel the garlic and slice very thinly. Heat 1 tablespoon of the oil in a pan, add the garlic and fry very briefly until it sizzles – be careful not to let it brown too much as it will make the dish taste bitter. Immediately add the remaining oil and vinegars to stop the cooking and swirl vigorously together.

Chop the sun-dried tomatoes; chop the capers coarsely. Swirl them into the dressing and season with pepper, adding a little salt only if needed. Pour the dressing over the salad.

Slice the omelettes into 0.5cm ribbons and curl them loosely over the beans.

Indian Spiced Fritters with Coriander Chutney

CALORIES PER SERVING: 215 (20 calories per fritter)

Serves 2 | Preparation time: 30 minutes, plus resting time | Cooking time: 10–20 minutes

Gently spiced veggies with a fresh chutney dip, this is irresistible Indian-style finger food.

275g vegetables, such
    as onion, cauliflower,
    carrots, green beans,
    red pepper
1 tsp cumin seeds
1 tsp coriander seeds
½ tsp chilli flakes
75g gram flour
1 tsp garam masala
½ tsp salt
1 tbsp vegetable oil

**for the coriander
chutney**

1 shallot, peeled
1 small garlic clove,
    peeled
1 hot red chilli
½ tsp salt
1 tbsp lime or lemon
    juice
65g roasted red pepper
    in oil, drained
2 tbsp chopped
    coriander

Prepare the vegetables: peel and roughly chop the onion; divide the cauliflower into small florets and halve; roughly chop the carrots and green beans; cut the red pepper into bite-sized pieces. Blanch in a pan of boiling water, until tender but with a slight bite.

Crush the cumin, coriander seeds and chilli flakes, using a pestle and mortar. Heat a frying pan, add the spices and fry for 2 minutes, stirring.

Mix the gram flour, garam masala and salt together in a bowl. Add the spice mixture, then gradually stir in about 75–100ml cold water, or enough to make a thick batter. Beat vigorously with a wooden spoon or a balloon whisk to remove any lumps. Leave the batter to stand for about 30 minutes.

Meanwhile, make the chutney. Quarter the shallot and place in a food processor or blender with all of the other ingredients, except the red pepper and coriander. Process until well mixed but still retaining some texture, then transfer to a bowl. Coarsely chop the red pepper and stir into the chutney along with the coriander. Cover and leave to stand for 30 minutes to let the flavours develop.

Heat the oil in a non-stick frying pan. Stir the vegetables into the batter. Place small spoonfuls of the battered veg in the frying pan and fry until golden underneath. Flip over and fry on the other side until golden and cooked through. Drain on kitchen paper and keep warm. Continue to cook until all the batter is used up, adding more oil to the pan as you need to – you should make about 20. Serve the spicy fritters piping hot with the coriander chutney.

Asian-style Chicken Noodle Soup

CALORIES PER SERVING: 229

Serves 2 | Preparation time: 15 minutes | Cooking time: 35 minutes

There's nothing more soothing and comforting than a steaming bowl of chicken noodle soup. Add more chilli if you like it fiery.

1 skinless chicken thigh, on the bone
1 lemon grass stalk, finely sliced
2.5cm piece fresh root ginger, cut into slivers
1 red chilli, sliced
1 garlic clove, sliced
50g egg noodles
1 carrot, cut into batons
3 stems purple sprouting broccoli or Tenderstem broccoli, roughly chopped
¼ red pepper, cut into strips
50g bean sprouts
1 tbsp miso paste
1 tsp sesame oil
1 spring onion, finely sliced, to garnish

Put the chicken, lemon grass, ginger, chilli and garlic in a pan with 600ml water. Cover and bring to the boil. Turn the heat right down low and simmer for 20 minutes.

Lift the chicken out of the pan and put on a board. Strain the stock into another pan, discard the aromatics, and add 300ml water. Shred the chicken.

Bring the stock up to the boil and add the noodles, carrot and broccoli. Simmer for 3 minutes.

Return the chicken to the pan and add the pepper and bean sprouts and stir in the miso paste. Simmer for another minute until the chicken is heated through and the veg is just tender.

Ladle between two bowls, stir in the sesame oil and sprinkle with the spring onion.

Beef Salad with a Sweet and Sour Dressing

CALORIES PER SERVING: 230

Serves 4 │ Preparation time: 35 minutes, plus marinating time │ Cooking time: 30–35 minutes

This recipe is based on a Thai dish called *larp*, which is similar to beef tartare. Here the beef is seared as a whole fillet, then sliced and served on a bed of tangy salad leaves.

225g fillet steak
1 tbsp Szechuan
    peppercorns
1 tsp ground black
    pepper
1 tsp ground coriander
¼ tsp Chinese five spice
125g salad leaves
1 tbsp sesame seeds
lime wedges, to serve

for the dressing
225g shallots, peeled
4 garlic cloves, peeled
2 large chillies,
    deseeded
2.5cm piece fresh root
    ginger, peeled
1 lemon grass stalk
1 tsp cumin seeds
3 tbsp sunflower oil
1 tbsp tamarind paste
1 tbsp light soy sauce or
    Thai fish sauce
2 tsp sugar

Preheat the oven to 200°C/400°F/Mark 6. Wash and dry the beef. Roughly grind the Szechuan peppercorns, using a pestle and mortar or spice grinder, and mix with the black pepper, ground coriander and five spice. Spread on a board. Press the steak down into the spice mixture, turning to coat well on both sides. Cover and leave to marinate in the fridge for 2 hours.

Meanwhile, prepare the dressing. Halve any large shallots; roughly chop the garlic, chillies and ginger; finely chop the lemon grass. Place these ingredients in a small roasting tin with the cumin seeds. Pour over the oil and toss well until evenly combined. Transfer to the oven and roast for 30 minutes until browned and softened. Allow to cool slightly.

Transfer the roasted aromatics to a food processor and add the tamarind paste, soy or fish sauce and the sugar. Purée to form a rough paste, adding a little water if it seems too thick. Taste and add a little salt if necessary.

Brush a griddle or heavy-based frying pan with a little oil and heat. As soon as the oil starts to smoke, add the beef fillet and sear by pressing down hard with a fish slice. Fry for 1 minute, turn the steak and repeat on the second side. Remove from the pan and leave to rest for 2 minutes.

Divide the salad leaves between individual serving plates. Thinly slice the beef fillet and arrange on the plates. Spoon on a little of the dressing and scatter over the sesame seeds. Serve at once, with lime wedges.

Baked Fennel with Lemon and Olives

CALORIES PER SERVING: 230

Serves 4 | Preparation time: 15 minutes | Cooking time: 45 minutes

Fennel bulbs are braised to tender sweetness with smoky black olives and lemon juice. This dish is equally delicious served hot or cold.

3 large fennel bulbs, or
    4 medium
grated zest and juice of
    1 lemon
6 tbsp olive oil
20 black or green olives
salt and pepper
2 tbsp chopped flat-leaf
    parsley, to garnish

Preheat the oven to 200°C/400°F/Mark 6. Trim the fennel and cut away any bruised parts. Cut off the fibrous tops, halve the bulbs lengthways and cut out the core. Cut larger bulbs into quarters.

Place the fennel halves or quarters cut-side up, in a baking dish. Mix the lemon zest and juice with the olive oil, salt and pepper.

Pour the lemon mixture over the fennel, scatter over the olives and bake in the oven for 15 minutes. Turn the fennel and bake for a further 15 minutes. Turn once more and bake for a final 15 minutes until tender. Serve sprinkled with the parsley.

Note: For a softer texture, blanch the fennel quarters in boiling water for 2 minutes and drain well before baking.

Mushroom and Artichoke Soup with Walnuts

(250)

CALORIES PER SERVING: 250

Serves 4 | Preparation time: 20 minutes, plus soaking time | Cooking time: 1½ hours

Jerusalem artichokes have a very distinctive flavour. The intense mushroom stock combines beautifully with the artichokes, and the walnuts add texture to the finished soup. This soup is great to freeze and can be cooked straight from frozen.

15g dried ceps
150ml boiling water
25g butter
1 tbsp chopped fresh
    thyme leaves
1 small onion, chopped
450g chestnut
    mushrooms,
    chopped
90ml dry sherry
1.2 litres vegetable stock
450g Jerusalem
    artichokes
1 garlic clove
2 tbsp walnut oil, plus
    extra to drizzle
25g walnuts, chopped
    and toasted
salt and pepper
thyme sprigs, to garnish

Put the dried ceps into a bowl, pour over the boiling water and let soak for 30 minutes. Drain, reserving the liquid.

Melt the butter in a saucepan, add the thyme and onion and fry gently for 10 minutes until soft but not browned. Increase the heat, add the chestnut mushrooms and ceps and stir-fry for 2 minutes. Add the sherry and boil rapidly until well reduced.

Add the vegetable stock and reserved cep stock and bring to the boil. Cover and simmer gently for 20 minutes until the stock is rich tasting and the mushrooms have lost all their flavour.

Meanwhile, scrub the artichokes and cut away the knobbly bits. Peel, then dice the flesh. Chop the garlic. Heat the oil in a large pan, add the artichokes and garlic and fry for 10 minutes, stirring, until evenly browned.

Strain the mushroom liquid through a fine sieve and add to the artichokes. Bring to the boil, cover and simmer for 35–40 minutes until the artichokes are cooked. Transfer to a blender or food processor and purée until very smooth.

Return the soup to the pan and heat gently for 5 minutes. Season with salt and pepper, to taste, and spoon into warmed soup bowls. Scatter the toasted nuts over the soup and drizzle with walnut oil. Serve at once, garnished with thyme.

Rocket and Goats' Cheese
with Roasted Pepper Salsa

CALORIES PER SERVING: 255

Serves 4 | Preparation time: 20 minutes | Cooking time: 25 minutes

Here a delicious juicy pepper salsa serves as the perfect partner for goats' cheese.
Roasting the peppers first not only sweetens them but also ensures that their skin
falls away from the flesh, making them far easier to peel.

1 small red pepper

1 small orange pepper

3 tbsp extra virgin olive
oil

1 small red onion

1 garlic clove

2 ripe plum tomatoes

1½ tbsp balsamic
vinegar

a pinch of sugar

2 tbsp chopped fresh
chervil

125g goats' cheese

125g rocket leaves

2 tbsp pine nuts,
toasted

salt and pepper

Preheat the oven to 230˚C/450˚F/Mark 8. Brush the
peppers with a little oil and place in a roasting tin. Roast in
the oven for 20 minutes, turning once, until charred. Transfer
to a bowl, cover with a tea towel and set aside until cool
enough to handle.

Carefully peel the peppers over the bowl, to catch the
juices, then discard the seeds. Dice the pepper flesh and
add to the juices.

Finely chop the onion and garlic. Immerse the tomatoes in
boiling water for 30 seconds, then remove and peel away
the skins. Halve, deseed and dice the tomato flesh.

Heat 1 tablespoon of the oil in a small pan, add the onion
and garlic and fry for about 3 minutes until softened. Add
the diced tomatoes and fry gently for a further 2 minutes.
Add to the peppers, toss to mix and set aside to cool.

Combine the remaining oil with the vinegar, sugar, chervil and
seasoning. Pour over the pepper mixture and toss to mix.

Thinly slice the goats' cheese. Divide the rocket between
individual serving plates and arrange the cheese in the
centre. Spoon some of the salsa over the cheese and drizzle
the rest liberally over the rocket. Scatter over the pine nuts
and serve at once.

Curried Carrot and Split Pea Soup

CALORIES PER SERVING: 260

Serves 4 | Preparation time: 35 minutes, plus soaking time | Cooking time: 1–1¼ hours

There is undoubtedly something particularly warming about a curried lentil or split pea soup. A tangy coriander and lime butter complements this soup perfectly, giving it a delicious finish. Alternatively you could omit the flavoured butter and simply sprinkle the soup with chopped coriander instead.

50g yellow split peas, soaked overnight in cold water
1 tbsp sunflower oil
1 small onion, chopped
1 garlic clove, chopped
I red chilli, deseeded and chopped
1 tsp grated fresh root ginger
1½ tsp hot curry paste
225g carrots, peeled and chopped
1 potato, peeled and chopped
salt and pepper

for the coriander and lime butter
50g butter, softened
grated zest and juice of 1 lime
1½ tsp chopped coriander

Drain the split peas, rinse well and place in a large saucepan with 1.5 litres of cold water. Bring to the boil and boil steadily for 10 minutes. Reduce the heat, cover and simmer gently for 30 minutes.

Meanwhile, make the coriander and lime butter. In a bowl, beat the butter with the lime zest and juice, coriander and a little pepper, until evenly combined. Form into a log shape on a piece of greaseproof paper, wrap in foil and chill in the fridge until required.

Heat the oil in a pan, add the onion, garlic, chilli and ginger and fry, stirring frequently, for 10 minutes until evenly browned. Stir in the curry paste, carrots and potato and fry for a further 5 minutes.

Add the curried vegetable mixture to the split peas. Return to the boil, cover and simmer for a further 35 minutes until the vegetables and peas are tender. Transfer to a blender or food processor and work until fairly smooth. Return to the pan, season with salt and pepper, to taste, and heat through.

Unwrap the butter and cut into thin slices. Pour the soup into warmed serving bowls and serve each portion topped with two slices of the flavoured butter.

Vegetable Couscous

CALORIES PER SERVING: 260

Serves 4 | Preparation time: 15 minutes | Cooking time: 15 minutes

For this quick Moroccan-style dish, couscous grains are steamed over a nourishing spicy vegetable stew. Use quick-cook couscous – which needs to be moistened before cooking but doesn't require lengthy soaking – and vary the vegetables as you like.

225g quick-cook couscous
225g aubergine
175g courgettes
175g carrots, peeled
1 large onion
1 tbsp oil
2 garlic cloves, crushed
2 tsp ground cumin
½ tsp mild chilli seasoning
½ tsp ground ginger
4 tbsp tomato purée
1 bay leaf
1 x 200g tin of chickpeas, drained
750ml vegetable stock
salt and pepper
chopped flat-leaf parsley, to garnish

Moisten the couscous according to the packet instructions. Cut the aubergine and courgettes into chunks. Chop the carrots. Finely chop the onion. Heat the oil in a saucepan (over which a steamer, metal sieve or colander will fit). Add the onion, carrots, garlic and spices and cook gently for 1 minute, stirring occasionally.

Add the tomato purée, bay leaf, aubergine, courgettes and chickpeas. Stir in the stock. Cover and bring to the boil, then uncover and boil rapidly for 8 minutes.

Meanwhile, fork the couscous to break up any lumps and spread in a steamer, metal sieve or colander lined with a double layer of muslin.

Place the couscous container over the cooking vegetables. Cover and cook for 5 minutes or until the vegetables are tender, the sauce is well reduced and the couscous is piping hot. Check the seasoning.

Spoon the couscous on to a warmed serving dish and fork through. Pile the vegetables and juices on top. Garnish with plenty of chopped parsley.

Roasted Aubergine with Flatbread

CALORIES PER SERVING: 265

Serves 4 │ Preparation time: 30 minutes, plus resting time │ Cooking time: 55 minutes

This spicy Middle Eastern-style salad is served with unleavened home-made bread.
If you haven't time to make your own bread, serve with lightly toasted pitta bread.

2 large aubergines, each
　　about 350g
4 tbsp olive oil
2 garlic cloves
1 onion
4 ripe plum tomatoes
¼ tsp turmeric
½ tsp ground coriander
a pinch of ground
　　cinnamon
a pinch of cayenne
　　pepper
grated zest and juice of
　　½ lemon
2 tbsp chopped
　　coriander
salt and pepper
coriander sprigs, to
　　garnish

for the bread

25g strong plain white
　　flour, plus extra for
　　rolling out
25g plain white flour
15g fine cornmeal
sesame and cumin
　　seeds, for sprinkling
olive oil, for brushing

Preheat the oven to 230°C/450°F/Mark 8. Halve the aubergines lengthwise, then score a criss-cross pattern over the cut surface. Sprinkle with 2 teaspoons of salt and set aside for 30 minutes. Rinse thoroughly and pat dry.

Place the aubergines in a roasting tin and brush the cut surfaces liberally with 2 tablespoons of the oil. Roast in the oven for 45–50 minutes until browned and soft, brushing occasionally with more oil. Allow to cool slightly.

Meanwhile, finely chop the garlic and onion. Immerse the tomatoes in boiling water for 30 seconds, then remove and peel; dice the flesh. Heat the remaining oil in a frying pan, add the garlic and onion and fry for 5 minutes. Add the tomatoes, spices and lemon zest, fry for 1 minute, then cover and simmer for 5 minutes. Stir in lemon juice to taste. Remove from the heat and set aside to cool.

Sift the flours, cornmeal and ¼ teaspoon of salt into a bowl and work in 3 tablespoons of warm water to form a firm dough. Knead lightly, divide into four pieces and place on a floured plate. Cover with cling film and rest for 30 minutes.

Brush a griddle or heavy-based frying pan liberally with oil. Roll out each piece of dough on a well-floured surface to a thin round about 3mm thick. Sprinkle with sesame and cumin seeds and roll firmly. Cook the breads, one at a time, on the heated griddle for 1 minute each side until speckled brown.

Serve the aubergines with the sauce on top, garnished with coriander and accompanied by the warm bread.

Hearty Cheese and Veg Salad

CALORIES PER SERVING: 268

Serves 2 | Preparation time: 10 minutes | Cooking time: 30–35 minutes

A very filling salad packed with texture and flavour – the seeds add a lovely crunch and the cheese is deliciously creamy.

½ butternut squash,
    peeled and chopped
1 red onion, roughly
    chopped
1 courgette, sliced into
    chunks
½ yellow pepper,
    deseeded and
    chopped into large
    pieces
2 garlic cloves,
    unpeeled
2 tsp olive oil
4 thyme sprigs
100g mixed salad leaves
1 tsp pumpkin seeds,
    toasted
100g reduced-fat
    Greek-style salad
    cheese, chopped
50g tinned chickpeas,
    drained
2 tsp red wine vinegar
salt and pepper

Preheat the oven to 200°C/400°F/Mark 6. Put all the vegetables and the garlic in a roasting tin. Drizzle 1 teaspoon of the oil over the vegetables then pour 200ml water into the bottom of the tin. Scatter over the thyme sprigs. Season well, toss everything together and roast for 30–35 minutes, until tender.

Put the salad leaves in a large bowl with the pumpkin seeds, cheese and chickpeas.

Whisk together the remaining oil and vinegar, and season. Add the roasted vegetables to the salad leaves, then drizzle over the dressing. Toss together and serve.

Mixed Bean Chilli

CALORIES PER SERVING: 270

Serves 6 | Preparation time: 20 minutes, plus soaking time | Cooking time: 2½–3 hours

A low-calorie version of a traditional Mexican chilli. Make a big batch and freeze it for up to three months. You can use tinned instead of dried beans. You will need one 425g tin of each. Rinse thoroughly and add 15 minutes before the end of the cooking time.

125g dried red kidney beans (or see above)

125g dried black-eye beans (or see above)

1 red onion

3 garlic cloves

2–3 dried hot red chillies

700g mixed vegetables, such as carrots, potatoes, peppers, aubergines

4 tbsp olive oil

1 tbsp mild paprika

1 tbsp tomato purée

2 tsp cumin seeds

2 bay leaves

1 cinnamon stick

1 x 400g tin chopped tomatoes

1 tbsp lime or lemon juice

a large handful of coriander

salt and pepper

Put the dried beans in separate bowls and pour on enough cold water to cover. Leave to soak overnight.

The next day, drain the beans, put them in separate pans and cover with cold water. Boil rapidly for 10 minutes, then lower the heat. Simmer until just tender: the red kidney beans will take 1–1½ hours; the black-eye beans 1½ hours. Add salt towards the end of the cooking time. Drain and rinse.

Finely chop the onion. Crush the garlic. Crumble the chillies, removing the seeds if a milder flavour is preferred. Peel and cut the vegetables into fairly large chunks.

Heat half of the oil in a large saucepan. Add the onion, half the garlic and half the chilli. Cook, stirring, for about 5 minutes, until the onion is softened. Add the paprika, tomato purée and cumin seeds and cook, stirring, for 2 minutes. Add the bay leaves, cinnamon stick, beans and prepared vegetables, stirring to coat in the onion mixture. Cook for 2 minutes, then add the tomatoes and about 150ml water. Bring to the boil, lower the heat and simmer for 45 minutes to 1 hour, until the vegetables are tender. If the mixture begins to stick, add a little extra water. About halfway through cooking, taste and add more chilli if necessary.

Meanwhile, whisk together the rest of the oil, lime or lemon juice and garlic. Roughly chop the coriander and stir into the oil mixture. Leave to stand while the chilli is cooking. When the chilli is ready, stir in the coriander mixture and check the seasoning.

Beef Satay

CALORIES PER SERVING: 273

Serves 2 │ Preparation time: 30 minutes, plus freezing and marinating time │
Cooking time: 30 minutes

This is a delicious Thai treat. Strips of beef are marinated for several hours, threaded on
to bamboo skewers and grilled until charred and tender. They are served with a peanut
dipping sauce and cubes of chilled cooked rice, which provide a cool, refreshing balance
to the spicy beef. Prepare the day before so the flavours have time to mingle.

175g fillet steak
1 garlic clove
1cm piece fresh root
    ginger, peeled
1 tbsp dark soy sauce
1 tbsp sweet sherry
½ tbsp rice or wine
    vinegar
1 tsp sesame oil
¼ tsp chilli powder

for the rice cubes
25g Thai fragrant rice
salt

for the peanut sauce
1 tbsp chopped
    unsalted peanuts
a good pinch of
    crushed chilli flakes
½ garlic clove, crushed
2 tsp dark soy sauce
2 tsp lime juice
½ tsp clear honey
25g coconut cream

Place the beef in the freezer for 15 minutes until firm. This
will make it easier to slice.

Using a sharp knife, slice the beef across the grain into thin
strips. Place in a shallow non-reactive dish. Crush the garlic
and grate the ginger; place in a bowl with the soy sauce,
sherry, vinegar, sesame oil and chilli powder. Pour over the
beef, stir well, cover and leave to marinate in a cool place for
2–4 hours.

Cook the rice in boiling salted water for 15 minutes until very
soft. Drain and refresh under cold water. Drain thoroughly.
Press the rice into a small oiled dish and smooth the surface.
Cover and chill in the fridge until required.

Preheat the grill to medium. Remove the beef from the
marinade and thread on to bamboo skewers in a zigzag
fashion. Place the beef skewers on the grill rack and grill as
close to the heat as possible for 4-5 minutes until tender,
turning halfway through cooking.

Meanwhile make the peanut sauce. Put the peanuts, chilli
flakes, garlic, soy sauce, lime juice and honey in a small pan
and heat gently. Add the creamed coconut and 50ml water
and cook over a gentle heat, stirring, until smooth. Remove
from the heat. Unmould the rice and cut into cubes. Serve
the beef satay with the peanut dipping sauce and rice cubes.

Grilled Prosciutto with Figs

CALORIES PER SERVING: 280

Serves 4 | Preparation time: 5 minutes | Cooking time: 5–10 minutes

This is a summery dish that should be made with very plump and sweet figs. The Parma ham is cooked but still juicy, while the figs are roasted until warm and caramelized.

8 fresh ripe figs
2 tbsp olive oil, for
   basting
12 thin slices of Parma
   ham
2 tbsp extra virgin olive
   oil, to drizzle
crushed black
   peppercorns
50g Parmesan cheese
   shavings

Stand each fig upright. Using a sharp knife, cut a cross through each top leaving the base of each fig intact. Ease the figs open and brush with olive oil.

Heat a griddle and when very hot, add the figs, cut-side down and cook for 5–10 minutes until hot and golden brown, turning once. Alternatively, place under a preheated searing hot grill and grill until browning and hot all the way through.

While the figs are cooking, place half the slices of Parma ham on the griddle and cook for 2–3 minutes until frazzled and starting to crisp. Remove and keep warm while cooking the remaining Parma ham. (Alternatively place under a very hot grill.)

Arrange 3 slices of Parma ham and 2 figs on each warmed serving plate. Drizzle with extra virgin olive oil and season with plenty of crushed black pepper. Scatter over the Parmesan shavings.

Chilli Chicken Wrap

CALORIES PER SERVING: 316

Serves 2 | Preparation time: 10 minutes | Cooking time: 3 minutes

This is a perfect quick lunch that can be packed into a lunchbox and taken to work. It's a great way of making use of leftovers, but you can also use slices of lean ready-roasted chicken.

1 tsp vegetable oil
100g leftover roast chicken, skin removed and shredded
½ red chilli, chopped
1cm piece fresh root ginger, chopped
1 garlic clove, sliced
juice of ½ lime
1 tsp dark soy sauce
2 tsp sesame oil
50g bean sprouts
1 carrot, grated
50g spinach
2 tortilla wraps
salt and pepper

Heat the vegetable oil in a non-stick frying pan or wok and add the chicken, chilli, ginger and garlic. Cook for 2–3 minutes until the chicken starts to turn golden and the garlic is cooked, but not brown.

Whisk together the lime juice, soy sauce and sesame oil with seasoning, to taste.

Divide the bean sprouts, grated carrot and spinach between two wraps, then top with the chicken. Drizzle over the dressing, roll up and tuck in!

Mexican Chicken

CALORIES PER SERVING: 325

Serves 6 │ Preparation time: 30 minutes, plus marinating time │ Cooking time: 15 minutes

This Mexican-style dish is bright and colourful – use different coloured peppers for maximum effect. Make a big batch and keep it in the fridge to serve with salads or tortillas with guacamole and salsa.

3 onions
2–3 hot chillies
2 garlic cloves, crushed
2 tbsp chopped
    coriander
grated zest and juice of
    2 limes
6 x 150g skinless
    chicken breasts
8 red, yellow or orange
    peppers (or a
    mixture)
1–2 tbsp olive oil
salt and pepper
coriander leaves, to
    garnish

Peel and halve the onions, leaving most of the root end attached so that they will hold their shape during cooking. Cut each half into wedges, working from the root end to the top. Slice the chillies, discarding the seeds if a milder flavour is preferred.

Put the garlic, onions, chillies, coriander, lime zest and juice in a shallow dish and mix thoroughly. Cut the chicken into large pieces and add to the dish. Stir well, cover and leave to marinate in a cool place for at least 1 hour or overnight.

Halve the peppers and remove the cores and seeds, then cut into wedges.

Heat the oil in a heavy-based frying pan. Remove the chicken and onions from the marinade with a slotted spoon, reserving the marinade. Add the chicken and onions to the pan and cook, turning, over a high heat until thoroughly browned on the outside. Remove the chicken from the pan.

Add the peppers to the pan and cook, turning, over a high heat for about 5 minutes until the onions and peppers are softened.

Return the chicken to the pan, add the marinade, lower the heat and cook for about 5 minutes, stirring occasionally, or until the chicken is cooked right through.

Season with salt and pepper, to taste, and sprinkle with the coriander leaves.

Pasta with Two-tomato Sauce

CALORIES PER SERVING: 340 if using regular pasta; 328 if using wholemeal pasta

Serves 6 | Preparation time: 15 minutes | Cooking time: 35–40 minutes

Made with fresh tomatoes and enriched with sun-dried tomato paste, this sauce makes a substantial meal served with pasta. Full-flavoured fresh ripe tomatoes give the best result but tinned plum tomatoes are a better choice than under-ripe or flavourless fresh ones. Make a large batch and freeze.

30g butter
1 small onion, chopped
2 garlic cloves, chopped
1kg ripe tomatoes,
    preferably plum,
    or two x 400g tins
    plum tomatoes with
    their juice
3 tbsp sun-dried tomato
    paste (see note)
2 oregano sprigs
400g dried fusilli,
    conchiglie or penne
25g freshly grated
    Parmesan cheese
salt and pepper
2 tbsp chopped flat-leaf
    parsley, to garnish

To prepare the sauce, melt the butter in a saucepan, add the onion and garlic and cook over a low heat for about 15 minutes while preparing the tomatoes. Add 2 tablespoons of water if the onions look like they're drying out.

If using fresh tomatoes, first skin them. Immerse in a bowl of boiling water for 30 seconds, then drain and refresh under cold running water. Peel away the skins. Quarter the tomatoes, discard the seeds, then roughly chop the flesh. If using tinned plum tomatoes, chop them roughly.

Add the tomatoes to the onion and garlic mixture together with the sun-dried tomato paste and oregano sprigs. Cook, uncovered, over a low heat for 25–30 minutes, stirring occasionally, until the sauce is thick and pulpy.

Meanwhile, cook the pasta in a large pan of boiling salted water until al dente or according to the packet instructions. Drain thoroughly in a colander.

Discard the oregano and season the sauce with salt and pepper, to taste. Add the pasta and toss well to mix. Serve at once, topped with the Parmesan and chopped parsley.

Note: You can buy sun-dried tomato paste, but it's also very easy to make. Simply use a food processor to purée the contents of a jar of sun-dried tomatoes in oil. Return the paste to the empty jar and store in the refrigerator until required.

Chicken, Potato and Spinach Frittata

345

CALORIES PER SERVING: 345

Serves 4 | Preparation time: 10 minutes | Cooking time: 20 minutes

For this tempting frittata choose waxy potatoes, which hold their shape when sautéed, and use a heavy-based frying pan to cook the frittata, or it will stick.

450g waxy potatoes
2 onions
220g cooked chicken or
    turkey
4 tbsp olive oil
1 garlic clove, crushed
a handful of baby
    spinach leaves
freshly grated nutmeg,
    to taste
5 large eggs, beaten
salt and pepper

Peel the potatoes and cut into 2.5cm chunks. Cut the onions in half, then slice. Cut the chicken or turkey into bite-sized pieces.

Heat half of the oil in a heavy-based, preferably non-stick, frying pan. Add the potatoes, onions and garlic. Cook over a high heat until the vegetables are tinged with brown. Reduce the heat and continue cooking, stirring occasionally, until the potatoes are cooked. If the mixture starts to stick, add a little more oil.

When the potatoes are cooked, add the chicken or turkey and cook over a high heat for 5 minutes or until the chicken is heated through. Add the spinach and cook until wilted, then season with salt, pepper and nutmeg.

Add a little extra oil to coat the bottom of the pan if necessary. Heat for 1 minute, then add the beaten eggs. Continue cooking over a high heat for about 2 minutes, to set the egg at the bottom, then lower the heat and cook until the egg at the top is just set.

Remove the pan from the heat. Using a palette knife, carefully loosen the frittata around the edge. Invert a plate over the pan, then turn the plate and pan over to release the frittata onto the plate. Slide the frittata back into the pan and cook for 1–2 minutes more.

Pasta Primavera

CALORIES PER SERVING: 348 per serving; 339 if using wholemeal pasta

Serves 2 | Preparation time: 10 minutes | Cooking time: 20 minutes

A healthy pasta dish that's chock full of fresh green spring vegetables. The pine nuts add a subtle creaminess to this very filling lunch.

100g farfalle
1 tsp olive oil
1 garlic clove, sliced
125g asparagus tips,
    halved
75g fine green beans,
    halved
100g shelled and
    skinned broad beans
50g peas
zest and juice of
    ½ lemon
2 tsp extra virgin olive oil
10g pine nuts, toasted
10g freshly grated
    Parmesan cheese
salt and pepper

Cook the pasta in a large pan of boiling water according to the packet instructions.

Meanwhile, in a large frying pan, heat the olive oil and cook the garlic for 1 minute. Add the vegetables and toss to coat in the garlic. Add a ladleful of the pasta cooking water, put the lid on and allow the vegetables to steam for 5–7 minutes until just tender.

Drain the pasta, leaving a little of the cooking water clinging to it. Add the lemon zest and juice to the vegetables, season and drizzle over the extra virgin olive oil. Stir to mix.

Add the vegetables to the pasta, then divide between two plates. Scatter over the pine nuts and Parmesan.

Kleftiko

CALORIES PER SERVING: 350

Serves 4 | Preparation time: 15 minutes, plus marinating time | Cooking time: 2–2½ hours

Kleftiko – or 'robber's lamb' as it is literally translated – is a traditional Greek recipe in which the lamb is seasoned with lemon and oregano and then cooked in a covered dish until meltingly tender.

8 lamb loin chops,
    or 4 leg steaks
    (with bone)
2 lemons
1 tbsp dried oregano
2 tbsp olive oil
2 onions
2 bay leaves
150ml dry white wine
150ml stock
salt and pepper
lemon wedges, to serve

Place the lamb in a single layer in a shallow dish. Squeeze the juice from the lemons into a small bowl or cup and add the oregano, salt and pepper. Sprinkle the mixture over the meat and leave to marinate in a cool place for at least 4 hours, preferably overnight.

Preheat the oven to 160°C/325°F/Mark 3. Heat the oil in a large frying pan. Lift the lamb chops out of the marinade and add them to the pan. Cook over a high heat, turning until well browned on all sides, then transfer to a shallow earthenware casserole.

Peel and slice the onions and add to the lamb, together with the bay leaves, wine and stock. Pour in any remaining marinade and season with pepper.

Cover the dish with foil. Bake in the oven for 2–2½ hours until the lamb is tender, removing the foil for the last 20 minutes to brown the meat.

Before serving, carefully skim off any excess fat. Serve the meat with the juices spooned over with lemon wedges on the side.

Stuffed Sardines

CALORIES PER SERVING: 365

Serves 4 | Preparation time: 25 minutes | Cooking time: 10 minutes

Fresh sardines are stuffed with a sweet and savoury mixture of pine nuts, parsley and raisins, then rolled and baked until tender.

16 fresh sardines
50g pine nuts, toasted
50g raisins
3 tbsp chopped flat-leaf parsley
finely grated zest and juice of 1 orange
100ml olive oil
salt and pepper

Preheat the oven to 180°C/350°F/Mark 4. Scrape the scales from the sardines if necessary, then cut off the heads. Slit open the bellies and clean the insides under cold running water. Lay, flesh-side down, on a board. Slide your thumb along the backbone, pressing firmly to release the flesh along its length. Take hold of the backbone at the head end and lift it out; the fish should now be open like a book.

For the stuffing, mix together the pine nuts, raisins, parsley, orange zest, and salt and pepper, to taste. Place a spoonful of stuffing on the flesh side of each fish. Roll up from the head end and secure with a cocktail stick if necessary.

Place the stuffed sardines in an oiled ovenproof dish into which they fit snugly. It is important that the sardines are tightly packed together. Pour over the orange juice and olive oil. Season with salt and pepper and bake for about 10 minutes.

Note: The cooking time will vary depending on the type of baking dish used. The sardines will cook more quickly in a thin metal baking tin than in a terracotta baking dish, for example. Avoid using frozen sardines as they have a disappointing flavour.

Pasta and Chickpea Soup with Rocket Pesto

CALORIES PER SERVING: 370

Serves 6 │ Preparation time: 25 minutes │ Cooking time: 1 hour

This soup is similar to minestrone with its selection of fresh green vegetables, but the pesto sauce is made with peppery rocket rather than the more usual basil, giving a cleaner taste to the finished soup. Make a large batch and then freeze before you add the pesto.

4 ripe tomatoes
3 tbsp olive oil
1 onion, chopped
2 garlic cloves, finely
    chopped
1 leek, trimmed and sliced
1 tbsp chopped rosemary
1 x 400g tin of chickpeas
1.2 litres vegetable stock
1 courgette, diced
125g shelled peas
125g French beans, halved
125g shelled and skinned
    broad beans
50g small pasta shells
2 tbsp chopped flat-leaf
    parsley
salt and pepper

for the rocket pesto
50g rocket
1 garlic clove, peeled
1 tbsp capers, rinsed and
    drained
1 tbsp chopped flat-leaf
    parsley
15g pine nuts, toasted
15g freshly grated
    Parmesan cheese
5 tbsp extra virgin olive oil

Immerse the tomatoes in a bowl of boiling water for 30 seconds, then remove with a slotted spoon and peel away the skins. Chop the tomato flesh.

Heat the oil in a large saucepan, add the onion, garlic, leek and rosemary and fry gently for 10 minutes until softened but not coloured. Add the chickpeas with their liquid, the stock and tomatoes. Bring to the boil, cover and simmer for 30 minutes.

Meanwhile make the rocket pesto. Wash and dry the rocket leaves and chop roughly. Place in a grinder or food processor and add the garlic, capers, parsley, pine nuts and Parmesan. Purée to form a fairly smooth paste, then stir in the oil and season with salt and pepper, to taste.

Add the courgette, peas and beans to the soup. Return to the boil and simmer for a further 10 minutes. Add the pasta and parsley and cook for 6–8 minutes until the pasta is al dente. Check and adjust the seasoning.

Serve the soup in warmed bowls with the rocket pesto spooned into the middle.

Hearty Stew

CALORIES PER SERVING: 390

Serves 6 │ Preparation time: 20 minutes │ Cooking time: 1 hour

This satisfying stew relies on a good mix of root vegetables to bolster up the chicken flavour. The split lentils thicken the liquid and heighten the robust feel of the meal. It's a great dish to freeze and have on standby.

1 x 1.4kg chicken (or chicken pieces)
2 tbsp plain white flour
2 tbsp olive oil
2 onions
2 parsnips
2 large carrots
2 large potatoes
125g split red lentils
2 bay leaves
2 garlic cloves
1 x 400g tin of black-eye or red kidney beans, drained
2 courgettes, sliced
3 tbsp chopped flat-leaf parsley
1 tbsp chopped fresh chives
salt and pepper

Joint the chicken into even-sized pieces. Sprinkle the chicken with flour and season with salt and pepper.

Heat the oil in a flameproof casserole and cook the chicken in batches until well browned on all sides. Remove from the casserole and set aside.

Meanwhile, roughly chop the onions. Peel the parsnips, carrots and potatoes; cut them all into chunks. Add a little extra oil to the casserole if necessary and cook the vegetables until lightly browned.

Return the chicken to the casserole and add the lentils, bay leaves, garlic and 900ml water. Cover with a tight-fitting lid and simmer gently, stirring occasionally, for 45 minutes or until the chicken is tender and the lentils are soft and mushy.

Rinse the beans and add to the casserole with the courgettes. Season to taste with salt and pepper. Cook for a further 15 minutes or until the courgettes are just tender and the beans are heated through. If the sauce is too thin, retrieve a few spoonfuls of vegetables, mash them with a potato masher and return to the stew to thicken it slightly. Sprinkle with the chopped parsley and chives.

Glazed Salmon with Soy and Ginger

CALORIES PER SERVING: 406

Serves 4 | Preparation time: 20 minutes | Cooking time: 10 minutes

Based on the Japanese teriyaki style of cooking, salmon fillets are marinated in a well-flavoured mixture that makes a shiny glaze once the fish is grilled.

6cm piece fresh root
    ginger
1 garlic clove, peeled
6 tbsp light soy sauce
8 tbsp mirin (Japanese
    rice wine) or sweet
    sherry
1 tbsp soft brown sugar
4 x 175g salmon fillets
200g pak choi

Crush the ginger and garlic using a pestle and mortar, until the juices start to run. Then, using your hands, squeeze out as much of the juice as possible into a shallow dish, taking care to exclude any solid pieces of ginger or garlic (as these would burn during cooking and spoil the effect).

Put the soy sauce, mirin and sugar into a small saucepan and dissolve over a low heat, then bring to the boil, stirring all the time. Boil for about 5 minutes until the mixture is slightly reduced and syrupy. Pour on to the ginger juice and leave to cool completely.

Add the fish to the dish and turn to coat with the marinade on all sides. Leave to marinate in a cool place for 30 minutes to 1 hour.

Preheat the grill to high. Thread the fish on to two long skewers. Thoroughly oil the grill pan and lay the fish in the pan, skin-side down. Grill for about 6–8 minutes or until the fish flakes easily when tested with a fork, brushing frequently during cooking with the excess marinade. If the salmon appears to be overcooking on the surface but not cooking underneath, lower the position of the grill pan rather than turn the fish over.

Steam the pak choi in a pan with a splash of water until tender. Serve with the salmon.

Mushroom and Parmesan Risotto

CALORIES PER SERVING: 420

Serves 4 | Preparation time: 15 minutes | Cooking time: 20 minutes

This is a wonderfully warming meal for a cold night. Make sure you pare the lemon rind in one large piece, so it's easy to remove.

1 lemon
175g flat mushrooms
175g French beans
225g broccoli florets
2 tbsp olive oil
1 medium onion, finely
    chopped
350g Arborio rice
a pinch of saffron
    threads (optional)
4 tbsp dry white wine
750ml vegetable stock
salt and pepper
1 tbsp finely shaved
    Parmesan cheese, to
    serve

Finely pare the rind from the lemon, using a vegetable peeler, then squeeze the juice. Wipe the mushrooms clean with a damp cloth, then slice.

Top and tail the French beans and cut in half lengthways. Blanch the broccoli and beans together in boiling salted water for 3–4 minutes. Drain and refresh under cold running water.

Heat the oil in a heavy-based saucepan or flameproof casserole and cook the onion gently for about 2–3 minutes until beginning to soften. Stir in the rice and saffron, if using. Season well and pour in the wine. Add the pared lemon rind, 2 tablespoons of lemon juice and the stock. Bring to the boil, stirring.

Cover and simmer the risotto for 5 minutes. Stir in the mushrooms, broccoli and French beans. Re-cover and simmer for a further 5 minutes, or until the rice is tender and most of the liquid is absorbed.

Discard the lemon rind and transfer the risotto to warmed serving plates. Top with slivers of Parmesan cheese and serve at once.

Tandoori Chicken with Minted Couscous

CALORIES PER SERVING: 440

Serves 6 | Preparation time: 20 minutes, plus marinating time | Cooking time: 20 minutes

The dressing for the couscous is sweet and balances the tangy chicken beautifully.
Make enough to serve six and have the rest for lunch or the following day.

6 x 125g skinless
    chicken breasts
275ml Greek-style
    yoghurt
2 garlic cloves, crushed
2.5cm piece fresh root
    ginger, peeled and
    grated
finely grated zest and
    juice of ½ lemon
2 tsp hot curry paste
1 tsp paprika
½ tsp salt
225g quick-cook
    couscous
4 ripe tomatoes,
    deseeded and diced
1 small red onion, finely
    chopped
lemon wedges and mint
    sprigs, to serve

for the dressing
juice of 2 lemons
25g caster sugar
25g mint leaves
125g cucumber
50g sultanas
4 tbsp extra virgin olive oil
salt and pepper

Wash and dry the chicken breast fillets and cut into 2.5cm cubes. Put the yoghurt in a large bowl with the garlic, ginger, lemon zest and juice, curry paste, paprika and salt. Add the chicken pieces, toss well to coat and leave to marinate in a cool place overnight.

The next day, wash the couscous to moisten and place in a muslin-lined steamer. Place over a pan of simmering water, cover with a tight-fitting lid and cook for 5–6 minutes until fluffy.

Meanwhile, prepare the dressing. Put the lemon juice and sugar in a saucepan and heat gently until dissolved. Stir in the remaining ingredients, seasoning to taste, and remove from the heat.

Transfer the couscous to a large bowl, add the dressing and stir with a fork until evenly mixed. Add the tomatoes and onion to the couscous, season to taste and set aside.

Preheat the grill. Remove the chicken from the marinade and thread onto 6 skewers. Grill for 10–15 minutes, turning frequently, until the chicken is charred on the outside and cooked right through. Leave to cool.

Spoon the couscous onto individual plates and top with the skewers. Garnish with lemon wedges and mint.

Note: If using bamboo skewers, pre-soak in cold water for 30 minutes to prevent them scorching under the grill.

Penne with Olives, Anchovy and Chilli

CALORIES PER SERVING: 445

Serves 6 | Preparation time: 10 minutes | Cooking time: 10 minutes

Use olives from the delicatessen that have been marinating in flavoured oils. They are usually far more delicious than olives found in jars and can be much cheaper. You won't need to add salt to this dish, as the ingredients themselves are naturally salty.

400g dried penne
2 garlic cloves
50g anchovies in olive oil
½ tsp dried chilli flakes
2 tbsp chopped flat-leaf
    parsley
230g stoned mixed black
    and green olives
4 tbsp extra virgin olive oil
2 tbsp freshly grated
    Parmesan cheese,
    plus extra to serve
pepper

Bring a large saucepan of salted water to the boil. Add the pasta and cook until al dente, or according to the packet instructions.

Meanwhile, thinly slice the garlic cloves. Place in a saucepan with the anchovies and their oil. Add the chilli flakes and cook over a fairly high heat for 2–3 minutes, stirring to break up the anchovies with a wooden spoon; do not allow the garlic to brown. Stir in the parsley and remove from the heat.

Transfer the contents of the pan to a food processor and add the olives and olive oil. Process for a few seconds to give a coarse paste. Season with pepper, to taste.

When the pasta is cooked, drain thoroughly in a colander. Return to the saucepan and add the pounded olive mixture and freshly grated Parmesan. Toss well to coat the pasta. Serve immediately, topped with a sprinkling of Parmesan shavings.

Lamb with Potato

CALORIES PER SERVING: 450

Serves 2 | Preparation time: 20 minutes | Cooking time: 1½ hours

Use waxy potatoes for this dish and don't cut them into small pieces or they will disintegrate during cooking.

1 hot red chilli
1 small onion, quartered
1 garlic clove
1cm piece fresh root
    ginger, peeled and
    roughly chopped
1 tbsp desiccated
    coconut
300g lean boneless lamb
200g waxy potatoes
1 tbsp ghee or
    vegetable oil
1 tsp paprika
½ tsp ground fenugreek
½ tsp ground turmeric
1 tsp ground coriander
½ tsp tsp ground cumin
50ml yoghurt
100ml meat or
    vegetable stock
salt and pepper

Preheat the oven to 180°C/350°F/Mark 4. Chop the chilli, discarding the seeds if a milder flavour is preferred. Put the onion, garlic, ginger, chilli and coconut in a blender with 1 tablespoon of water and process until smooth.

Trim the meat of any excess fat and cut into 4cm cubes. Peel the potatoes and cut into large chunks.

Heat the ghee or oil in a flameproof casserole, add the onion paste and cook until golden brown, stirring all the time. Add the spices and cook, stirring, over a high heat for 2 minutes.

Brown the meat and potatoes in the casserole over a high heat, in batches if necessary, turning constantly until thoroughly browned on all sides. Lower the heat and return all the meat and potatoes to the casserole. Add the yoghurt, a spoonful at a time, stirring after each addition.

Add the stock and season liberally with salt. Bring to the boil, then reduce the heat, cover and cook in the oven for about 2 hours or until the meat is very tender.

When the meat and potatoes are tender, remove with a slotted spoon; set aside. Bring the sauce to the boil and boil steadily until the sauce is well reduced and very thick. Return the meat and potatoes to the casserole and stir to coat with the sauce.

dinner

Thai Fishcakes

CALORIES PER FISCAKE: 100

Makes 10 | Preparation time: 25 minutes | Cooking time: 20 minutes

Bursting with strong flavours from the chillies, Kaffir lime leaves and lemon grass, these bear absolutely no resemblance to the traditional British fishcake! Serve them on a bed of crunchy fresh salad leaves. This recipe makes 10, so freeze any you aren't planning on using immediately.

450g white fish fillets, such as cod or haddock

4 Kaffir lime leaves

2 tbsp chopped coriander

1 tbsp Thai fish sauce

1 tbsp lime juice

2 tbsp Thai red curry paste

salt and pepper

flour, for coating

vegetable oil, for shallow-frying

to serve

mixed salad leaves

shredded spring onion

1 mild red chilli, sliced

lime wedges

Remove any skin and pin bones from the fish, then place the fish in a food processor or blender and work until smooth.

Finely chop the lime leaves and add to the fish with the coriander, fish sauce, lime juice and red curry paste. Season with salt and pepper. Process until well mixed.

Using lightly floured hands, divide the mixture into 10 pieces and shape each one into a cake, about 6cm in diameter.

Shallow-fry the fishcakes in batches. Heat a 1cm depth of oil in a frying pan. Cook the fishcakes, a few at a time, for about 4 minutes each side. Drain on crumpled kitchen paper and keep hot while cooking the remainder.

Serve the fishcakes as soon as they are all cooked, on a bed of salad leaves scattered with shredded spring onion and chilli slices. Serve with lime wedges.

Vegetable, Noodle and Tofu Broth

CALORIES PER SERVING: 130

Serves 4 | Preparation time: 20 minutes | Cooking time: 1¼ hours

The success of this soup depends on the quality of the stock, which is used to poach a selection of vegetables and the tofu. The following recipe gives an authentic Thai stock – make a large batch and freeze the stock to use in this or other soups.

25g dried black or
    shiitake mushrooms
1 large carrot
50g cauliflower florets
50g baby sweetcorn
100g plain tofu
2 tbsp dark soy sauce
1 tbsp lemon or lime juice
50g dried egg thread
    noodles
mint leaves, to serve
chilli oil, to serve

for the Thai-style stock
1 onion, roughly chopped
2 carrots, roughly
    chopped
2 celery sticks, roughly
    chopped
2 garlic cloves, roughly
    chopped
2 lemon grass stalks,
    roughly chopped
15g fresh root ginger,
    roughly chopped
4 Kaffir lime leaves
4 coriander roots,
    scrubbed
1 tsp white peppercorns
1 tsp salt

Start by making the stock. Place 1.2 litres water in a large saucepan and add the onion, carrots, celery, garlic, lemon grass and ginger. Scatter over the remaining ingredients, bring to the boil, cover and simmer over a gentle heat for 1 hour.

Put the dried mushrooms in a bowl, pour over 120ml boiling water and leave to soak for 30 minutes. Strain and reserve the liquid; chop the mushrooms.

Prepare the remaining vegetables. Cut the carrot into matchsticks; divide the cauliflower into small florets; halve the sweetcorn lengthways; set aside. Cube the tofu.

Strain the stock into a clean pan and stir in the soy sauce, lemon or lime juice and reserved mushroom liquid. Return to the boil and stir in the prepared vegetables, tofu and soaked mushrooms. Simmer for 5 minutes.

Plunge in the noodles and simmer for a further 5–6 minutes until the noodles and vegetables are tender. Ladle the soup into large warmed soup bowls. Serve at once, scattered with mint leaves and drizzled with a little chilli oil.

Grilled Stuffed Peppers

CALORIES PER SERVING: 135

Serves 4 | Preparation time: 20 minutes | Cooking time: 20 minutes

A colourful salad full of flavours evocative of the Mediterranean – smoky grilled peppers, aromatic fennel and garlic, and a sweet balsamic vinegar dressing.

2 small onions
2 red peppers
2 yellow peppers
2 garlic cloves, peeled
2 tbsp capers
1 tbsp fennel seeds
3½ tbsp olive oil
1½ tbsp balsamic
    vinegar
2 tbsp roughly torn
    flat-leaf parsley
coarse sea salt and
    pepper

Peel the onions, leaving the root end intact, and cut into quarters. Drop them into a pan of boiling water and cook for 1 minute; drain well.

Preheat the grill to high. Halve the peppers lengthwise cutting through the stems, then core and deseed them. Arrange on the grill rack, skin-side up, in a single layer (you may need to do this in two batches). Place the onion quarters and garlic cloves on the rack too. Grill until the pepper skins are blistered and well charred. Turn the onions and garlic as necessary, but let them char slightly too.

Place the peppers in a bowl, cover with a plate and allow to cool slightly, then peel away their skins. Arrange the peppers on a serving platter. Fill the cavities with the grilled onions and capers.

Put the fennel seeds in a dry frying pan and toast over a medium heat for a few minutes until they begin to pop and release their aroma. Transfer to a mortar and pestle and coarsely grind them. Add the grilled garlic and grind to a paste. Transfer the garlic paste to a small bowl and whisk in the oil and vinegar.

Sprinkle the parsley, sea salt and pepper over the salad and spoon on the dressing. Serve at room temperature.

Salad of Bayonne Ham, Melon and Artichokes

CALORIES PER SERVING: 143

Serves 4 | Preparation time: 35 minutes | Cooking time: 10 minutes

In France, country or mountain hams are dried and sometimes smoked, too. They are typically served in thick slices as part of a salad or *assiette de charcuterie*. Here the classic combination of salty ham and sweet juicy melon is enhanced with tender young artichoke hearts and a herb vinaigrette.

8 fresh baby artichokes
lemon juice, for
    brushing
1 tbsp olive oil
½ ripe orange-fleshed
    melon, such as
    charentais or
    cantaloupe
4 thick slices Bayonne
    or Parma ham
salt and pepper
mixed salad leaves and
    herb sprigs, to serve

for the herb vinaigrette
2 tsp red wine vinegar
1 tsp Dijon mustard
2 tbsp olive oil
1 tbsp chopped chervil
    or tarragon
r

To prepare the artichokes, break off the tough outer leaves at the base until you expose a central core of pale leaves. Slice off the tough green or purple tips. Using a small sharp knife, pare the dark green skin from the base and down the stem. Brush the cut parts with lemon juice to prevent browning. Cut into quarters and brush with lemon juice.

Heat the oil in a sauté pan or heavy-based frying pan. Add the artichokes and cook over a high heat, stirring constantly, until they are just turning brown. Transfer to a bowl and allow to cool. Season with salt and pepper.

Halve the melon and scoop out the seeds. Either scoop the flesh into balls, cut into cubes or skin and slice thinly. Place the melon in the bowl with the artichokes. Toss lightly to mix.

Whisk all the ingredients for the dressing together until evenly amalgamated. Season with salt and pepper, to taste. Pour over the artichokes and melon and turn to coat.

Using a sharp knife, slice the ham into strips and add to the melon and artichokes. Arrange a few salad leaves on each individual serving plate and spoon the salad on top. Garnish with herb sprigs and serve immediately.

Note: Be sure to choose a fully ripe melon. A sweet, perfumed aroma is the best indicator of ripeness. If fresh baby artichokes are unobtainable, use 12 frozen prepared artichoke hearts instead; defrost thoroughly before use.

Spiced Lentil Soup

CALORIES PER SERVING: 148

Serves 2 | Preparation time: 5 minutes | Cooking time: 20 minutes

Sweet potato, carrots and red lentils give this warming soup a vibrant and uplifting colour. The chilli and spices add a touch of heat – add a little more chilli if you prefer it a bit hotter.

1 sweet potato, peeled
    and chopped
1 carrot, chopped
2 tbsp split red lentils
500ml vegetable stock
½ red chilli, chopped
¼ tsp cumin seeds
¼ tsp ground coriander
salt and pepper
a squeeze of lemon
    juice, to serve

Place the sweet potato and carrot in a saucepan. Add the red lentils, stock, chilli, cumin seeds and ground coriander. Season well with salt and pepper.

Cover the pan and bring to the boil. Once it's boiling, turn the heat down low and simmer for 10 minutes, until the lentils are soft.

Purée the soup, check and adjust the seasoning and squeeze over the lemon juice.

Thai Mussel Salad

CALORIES SERVING: 156

Serves 2 | Preparation time: 25 minutes | Cooking time: 10 minutes

Succulent mussels – fragrant with Thai flavourings – are served on a nest of vegetable ribbons and frisée. If time permits, soak the mussels in a bowl of cold water with a handful of oatmeal added for several hours before cooking to help rid them of any grit.

1 small carrot, cut into
    thin batons
1 small courgette, cut into
    thin batons
½ small fennel bulb,
    finely sliced
1 tsp salt
250g live mussels
1 tsp vegetable oil
50g frisée (curly endive)
a handful of Thai basil
    leaves or celery
    leaves, to serve

for the stock
1 garlic clove, peeled
1cm fresh root ginger,
    peeled and sliced
1 Kaffir lime leaf, bruised
1 lemon grass stalk,
    bruised
1 red chilli, bruised
½ tbsp Thai fish sauce

for the dressing
2 tbsp lime juice
1 tbsp rice wine vinegar
10g caster sugar
½ tsp crushed red chillies
¼ tsp salt

Place the carrot, courgette and fennel in a colander and sprinkle with the salt. Set aside to drain for 30 minutes.

In the meantime, scrub the mussels thoroughly under cold running water and pull away any straggly beards. Discard any opened mussels that do not close when tapped firmly.

Place all the stock ingredients in a saucepan with 150ml cold water. Bring to the boil, cover and simmer for 10 minutes, then strain into a clean pan.

Add the mussels to the stock, bring to the boil, cover and cook over a high heat for 4–5 minutes or until the shells have opened. Discard any mussels that remain closed. Strain, reserving the liquid, and immediately refresh the mussels under cold running water. Drain and set aside.

Place 3 tablespoons of the reserved mussel liquid in a pan. Add the dressing ingredients, heat gently to dissolve the sugar, then keep warm.

Wash the vegetables to remove the salt and pat dry thoroughly with kitchen paper.

Heat the vegetable oil in a wok and fry the vegetables in batches for 2–3 minutes until golden.

Divide the frisée between serving plates, top with the vegetables and sit the mussels on top. Spoon over the warm dressing and serve at once, garnished with Thai basil leaves.

Prawns with Spinach

CALORIES PER SERVING: 162

Serves 4 | Preparation time: 25 minutes | Cooking time: 15 minutes

Fresh spinach gives this dish a wonderful vibrance and it contrasts wonderfully with the creamy prawns. Most coconut milk comes in 400ml tins, but you can freeze the remaining 200ml for up to a month.

700g large raw prawns
    in shells
450g spinach
2 tbsp vegetable oil
1 medium onion, sliced
1 garlic clove, sliced
5cm piece fresh root
    ginger, peeled and
    cut into thin strips
2 tsp ground turmeric
1 tsp chilli powder
1 tbsp black mustard
    seeds
2 tsp ground coriander
a large pinch of ground
    cloves
200ml reduced-fat
    coconut milk
1 tbsp lime or lemon
    juice
salt

To prepare the raw prawns, remove the heads, if necessary, then peel off the shell leaving the fan-like piece at the end of the tail attached. Using a small sharp knife, make a shallow slit along the back of each prawn and remove the dark intestinal vein. Rinse the prawns under cold running water. Drain and pat dry with kitchen paper.

Trim the spinach leaves and wash thoroughly in several changes of water if necessary; drain well.

Heat the oil in a large frying pan or wok. Add the onion, garlic and ginger and fry, stirring, until softened. Add the spices and cook for 2 minutes, stirring all the time.

Add the coconut milk, bring to the boil, then lower the heat and simmer for 5 minutes. Add the prawns and simmer for about 4 minutes or until they just begin to look opaque.

Add the spinach; it may be difficult to fit it all in but don't worry, it will reduce down as it cooks in the steam. Cover the pan with a lid or a baking tray and cook for about 3 minutes or until the spinach is wilted; don't keep removing the lid to check during cooking or you will let the steam escape. Stir the wilted spinach into the sauce, add the lime or lemon juice and serve.

Crab Salad

CALORIES PER SERVING: 168

Serves 6 | Preparation time: 20 minutes | Cooking time: 3 minutes

There is nothing quite like the taste of freshly cooked crab meat and this salad is the perfect way to appreciate it. If you are lucky enough to obtain fresh cooked crabs you will need two, each about 1.4kg. The dark meat is not included in this dish but it can be frozen for future use.

450g white crab meat
6 spring onions, trimmed
2 tbsp chopped
    coriander
1 tbsp chopped chives
a pinch of cayenne
    pepper
2 garlic cloves
2.5cm piece fresh root
    ginger, peeled
2 tbsp vegetable oil
2 Kaffir lime leaves,
    shredded
½ tsp dried crushed chilli
    flakes
4 tbsp lime juice
1 tbsp sugar
1 tsp shrimp paste
1 tbsp Thai fish sauce or
    soy sauce
2 heads of radicchio or
    red chicory
50g cucumber
25g bean sprouts
1 carrot, finely sliced
lime wedges, to serve
a handful of coriander
    leaves, to serve

Flake the white crab meat into shreds and place in a bowl. Finely chop the spring onions and add to the crab with the coriander, chives and cayenne pepper. Mix gently, then cover and chill until required.

Crush the garlic and ginger together, using a pestle and mortar. Heat the oil in a small pan, add the garlic, ginger, lime leaves and chilli flakes and fry over a gentle heat for 3 minutes until softened but not brown. Add the lime juice, sugar, shrimp paste and fish sauce. Stir well, then remove from the heat. Leave to cool.

Drizzle the cooled dressing over the crab mixture and toss lightly until evenly combined. Arrange the radicchio or chicory leaves on serving plates and spoon over the crab mixture. Thinly slice the cucumber and arrange on top of each serving with the bean sprouts and carrot. Garnish with lime wedges and coriander leaves.

Glazed Chicken Wings

CALORIES PER SERVING: 175

Serves 4 | Preparation time: 10 minutes, plus marinating time | Cooking time: 1 hour

The spices and flavourings in this recipe make a rich glaze for the chicken wings. It is simple and quick to prepare, but the longer the wings are left to marinate the more flavour they absorb.

12 small chicken wings
4 garlic cloves
2 tsp hot chilli sauce
3 tbsp sweet soy sauce
1 tbsp preserved stem
    ginger syrup or clear
    honey
1 tbsp lemon juice
1 tsp ground coriander
½ tsp ground cinnamon
2 spring onions,
    shredded, to serve
lime or lemon wedges,
    to serve

Wash and dry the chicken wings. Tuck the tip of each wing under the thickest part of the wing, forming a triangular shape. Transfer to a large shallow, non-reactive dish.

Crush the garlic and place in a bowl. Add all the remaining ingredients, mix well, then pour over the chicken wings. Toss to coat the wings thoroughly. Cover and leave to marinate in a cool place for at least 4 hours, preferably overnight.

Preheat the oven to 220°C/425°F/Mark 7. Transfer the chicken wings and marinade juices to a roasting tin just large enough to hold them in a single layer. Bake at the top of the oven for about an hour, basting and turning frequently until the wings are glazed and tender. The flesh should almost fall from the bone. Serve hot, with spring onion shreds and lime and/or lemon wedges. Remember to provide finger bowls.

Roasted Tomatoes with a Garlic Crust

CALORIES PER SERVING: 185

Serves 6 | Preparation time: 15 minutes | Cooking time: 20 minutes

In this easy adaptation of the classic stuffed tomato, flavourful cherry or other small tomatoes are baked whole under a delicious crust of chopped garlic, parsley, toasted breadcrumbs and olive oil.

6 slices day-old stale
    bread
6 garlic cloves
3 tbsp chopped fresh
    parsley, plus extra to
    garnish
700g cherry tomatoes
olive oil, for basting
salt and pepper

Preheat the oven to 220°C/425°F/Mark 7. Tear up the bread and place in a food processor or blender. Process until you have fine breadcrumbs; there should be approximately 125g. Place in a heavy-based frying pan and dry-fry over a moderate heat until golden.

Finely chop the garlic. Stir into the breadcrumbs with the chopped parsley and salt and pepper to taste.

Place the tomatoes in a shallow roasting tin or dish, positioning them close together and in a single layer. Sprinkle the breadcrumbs evenly over the tomatoes and drizzle with olive oil.

Bake in the oven for 15–20 minutes until the crust is golden and the tomatoes are soft. The tomatoes will have disintegrated slightly under the crust. Scatter with more parsley to serve.

Butternut Squash Soup with Parmesan Crostini

CALORIES PER SERVING: 185

Serves 4 | Preparation time: 40 minutes | Cooking time: 50 minutes

Creamy butternut is ideal for puréeing, and both the sharpness of the Parmesan and the crisp bite of the crostini set it off beautifully to produce a really special soup. It also freezes well, so store some away for a cold night.

2 tbsp olive oil
1 large leek, trimmed
    and sliced thickly
1 celery stick, chopped
1 garlic clove chopped
1 tbsp chopped fresh
    sage
1 small red chilli, halved
    and deseeded
350g peeled, deseeded
    butternut squash
    and diced (see note)
1 litre vegetable stock
a pinch of cayenne
    pepper
salt and pepper

for the Parmesan crostini

4 thin slices day-old
    ciabatta or French
    bread
2 garlic cloves, peeled
25g Parmesan cheese
extra virgin olive oil, for
    drizzling

Preheat the oven to 200°C/400°F/Mark 6. Heat the oil in a saucepan, add the leek, celery and garlic and fry gently for 10 minutes. Add the sage, chilli and squash, and stir-fry for 5 minutes until the squash begins to colour.

Pour in the stock, add the cayenne and bring to the boil. Cover and simmer for 35 minutes, then transfer to a food processor and blend until smooth. Return to the pan, adjust the seasoning and heat through.

Meanwhile, make the crostini. Place the bread on a baking sheet and bake in the oven for 10 minutes. Rub each side with garlic, drizzle with a little oil and return to the oven for a further 10 minutes or until the bread is crisp and golden.

Spoon the soup into warmed bowls, and top with the crostini. Grate over the Parmesan and drizzle over a little more oil. Serve at once.

Note: To give this prepared weight of squash you will need about 450g.

Lemon Chicken

CALORIES PER SERVING: 190

Serves 4 | Preparation time: 20 minutes, plus marinating time | Cooking time: 45 minutes

Corn-fed chicken pieces are marinated in lemon juice, chilli and garlic, with a touch of honey. Ripe, juicy lemon halves are tucked in and around the joints to impart extra flavour during roasting.

1 x 1.6 kg corn-fed
    chicken, or 4 large
    chicken joints
4 really ripe juicy
    lemons
8 garlic cloves
2 small red chillies,
    halved and
    deseeded
1 tbsp honey
4 tbsp chopped flat-leaf
    parsley
salt and pepper

Using a sharp knife and/or poultry shears, cut the whole chicken, if using, into 8 small or 4 large joints. Place the chicken joints, skin-side down, in a large shallow ovenproof baking dish.

Halve the lemons, squeeze the juice and pour into a small bowl; reserve the empty lemon halves.

Crush two of the garlic cloves and add to the lemon juice. Add the chillies and honey. Stir well, pour over the chicken and tuck the lemon halves around. Cover and leave to marinate for at least 2 hours, turning once or twice.

Preheat the oven to 200°C/400°F/Mark 6. Turn the chicken skin-side up. Halve the rest of the garlic cloves and scatter over the chicken. Roast in the oven for 45 minutes or until golden brown and tender. Stir in the parsley and season with salt and pepper, to taste. Serve hot, garnished with the roasted lemon halves.

Tomato and Peach Salad with Avocado Salsa

CALORIES PER SERVING: 195

Serves 4 │ Preparation time: 15 minutes │ Cooking time: 3 minutes

This is a really attractive platter – add a few chive flowers or decorative edible leaves if you have any growing close at hand.

1 large ripe beef tomato
2 large firm ripe
  peaches
chopped chives, to serve
coriander sprigs, to
  serve
lime wedges, to serve

for the avocado salsa
½ small ripe avocado
2 spring onions,
  trimmed
1 small red chilli
1 garlic clove, crushed
1½ tsp lime juice
1½ tsp chopped
  coriander
1½ tsp extra virgin olive oil
salt and pepper

for the dressing
1 tbsp caster sugar
1 tsp lemon juice
½ tsp Dijon mustard
2 tbsp extra virgin olive oil

First prepare the avocado salsa. Peel and dice the avocado, finely slice the spring onions; halve, deseed and finely chop the chilli. Mix these ingredients together in a bowl and stir in the garlic, lime juice, coriander and oil. Season with salt and pepper, to taste, and set aside until required.

To prepare the dressing, dissolve the sugar in 50ml water in a small pan over a low heat. Bring to the boil and simmer for 3 minutes. Remove from the heat, allow to cool, then stir in the lemon juice and mustard. Gradually whisk in the oil until amalgamated and add seasoning, to taste.

Thinly slice the tomato. Halve, stone and slice the peaches. Scatter the tomato and peach slices on a large plate.

Spoon over the avocado salsa and drizzle over the dressing. Sprinkle with chives and garnish with coriander sprigs and lime wedges. Serve at once.

Note: Allow the salsa to stand while preparing the rest of the salad, but no longer or the avocado will discolour and spoil the appearance of the dish.

Chinese Beef

CALORIES PER SERVING: 200

Serves 4 | Preparation time: 20 minutes, plus marinating time | Cooking time: 15 minutes

Quickly cooked in very little oil, the natural flavours and textures of the vegetables in this dish are retained. Tender strips of beef are marinated in a rich sauce of black and yellow bean sauce.

350g fillet steak
2 bunches of spring
    onions
2 orange peppers
1 red chilli
225g broccoli
175g spinach (or pak
    choi)
1 tbsp chilli oil

for the marinade
2 tbsp sherry vinegar
2 tbsp black bean sauce
2 tbsp yellow bean
    sauce
2.5cm piece fresh root
    ginger
1 tbsp dark soy sauce

First, prepare the marinade. Mix the sherry vinegar with the black and yellow bean sauces. Peel and crush the ginger and add to the mixture with the soy sauce.

Slice the fillet steak into thin strips, about 5cm long and 1cm wide. Stir into the marinade. Cover and leave to marinate in a cool place for at least 30 minutes or up to 12 hours in the fridge.

Trim the spring onions and cut into diagonal strips about 5cm long. Cut the peppers and chilli in half, remove and discard the seeds. Slice the peppers into thin strips; cut the chilli into very fine strips. Cut the broccoli into small even florets. Shred the spinach.

Drain the meat from the marinade, using a slotted spoon. Heat the oil in a large non-stick frying pan or wok over a hight heat, add the meat and cook for 3–4 minutes, stirring. Stir in the vegetables and cook for 3–4 minutes. Stir in the marinade and heat through for 3–4 minutes. Serve immediately.

Lime-marinated Halibut
with Avocado and Red Onion Salsa

CALORIES PER SERVING: 210

Serves 4 | Preparation time: 10 minutes, plus marinating

This recipe is based on the famous South American dish ceviche – raw fish marinated in citrus juices. The acid from the fruit 'cooks' the fish, but retains the texture, keeping it moist. Your fish must be very fresh.

575g halibut
juice of 1 orange
juice of 5 limes

for the salsa
1 red pepper
1 red chilli
1 small red onion
1 beef tomato
1 small avocado
4 tbsp chopped
    coriander
2 tbsp chopped flat-leaf
    parsley
¼ tsp salt
pepper

Remove any skin and bones from the fish, and cut into bite-sized pieces. Place in a bowl with the orange juice and lime juice. Turn the fish and make sure that it is all covered with citrus juice. Cover the bowl and leave to marinate in the refrigerator for at least 8 hours, or preferably overnight.

To make the salsa, halve the pepper, remove the core and seeds, then dice the flesh. Cut the chilli in half lengthways, remove the seeds and chop very finely. Peel and dice the red onion. Mix all these ingredients together in a bowl.

Immerse the tomato in a small bowl of boiling water, leave for 30 seconds, then refresh in cold water. Peel away the skin. Cut the tomato into quarters, remove the seeds, then dice the flesh.

Cut the avocado in half, remove the stone and peel away the skin. Cut the flesh into dice. Add to the onion mixture with the tomato, coriander, parsley, and salt and pepper to taste. Mix together well. Serve the marinated fish on individual plates topped with a spoonful of salsa.

Note: If a smoother sauce is preferred, the salsa ingredients can be puréed in a blender or food processor.

Minted Lamb Escalopes

CALORIES PER SERVING: 210

Serves 6 | Preparation time: 10 minutes, plus marinating time | Cooking time: 6 minutes

Extra-lean, wafer-thin lamb escalopes are flavoured with a fresh-tasting minted yoghurt marinade, then grilled to perfection.

450g lean lamb
    escalopes
¼ red onion, finely
    sliced
40g baby spinach
12 cherry tomatoes,
    halved
1 tbsp mint leaves, to
    garnish

for the marinade
6 slightly heaped tbsp
    Greek-style yoghurt
1 garlic clove, crushed
4 tbsp chopped mint
2 tbsp lemon juice
salt and pepper

For the marinade, mix the yoghurt, crushed garlic, chopped mint and lemon juice together in a shallow non-metallic dish. Season with salt and pepper. Add the lamb escalopes and turn to coat evenly. Cover the dish and leave to marinate in a cool place for 2–3 hours.

Preheat the grill to high. Place the lamb escalopes on the grill rack in a single layer. Grill for 3 minutes on each side or until golden brown and cooked through, basting occasionally with the marinade.

Slice the lamb. Toss the red onion, spinach and tomatoes together, then divide among serving plates. Top with the lamb and mint leaves.

Vegetable Rice Noodles with Omelette Strips

CALORIES PER SERVING: 230

Serves 4 | Preparation time: 20 minutes | Cooking time: 10 minutes

Transparent noodles are tossed with stir-fried vegetables and topped with coriander omelette shreds.

2.5cm piece fresh root
   ginger
175g shiitake or button
   mushrooms
30g Chinese leaves
1 red chilli
125g rice noodles
1 tsp vegetable oil
1 tbsp groundnut oil
125g mangetout
75g bean sprouts
2 tbsp dark soy sauce
2 tbsp dry sherry
1 tsp sugar

for the omelette
2 medium eggs
2 tbsp semi-skimmed
   milk
3 tbsp chopped
   coriander
1 tsp vegetable oil
salt and pepper

To make the omelette, put the eggs, milk, coriander and seasoning in a jug and whisk together, using a fork.

Heat the oil in an omelette pan or small frying pan. Pour in the egg mixture and cook over a high heat until it begins to set. As it sets around the edge, use a palette knife to pull the set mixture towards the middle, letting the uncooked mixture run underneath. Cook until the egg is set all over.

Turn the omelette out onto a sheet of non-stick baking parchment and leave to cool. When cool, roll up and cut into thin slices.

Peel and shred the ginger. Thickly slice the mushrooms. Coarsely shred the Chinese leaves. Slice the chilli, removing the seeds if a milder flavour is preferred.

Cook the noodles according to the instructions on the packet. Drain well and toss in a little vegetable oil.

Heat the groundnut oil in a wok. Add the mushrooms and ginger and stir-fry over a high heat for 2 minutes. Add the chilli, mangetout, bean sprouts and shredded leaves and stir-fry for 1 minute. Add the soy sauce, sherry and sugar and cook for 1 minute to heat through. Add the noodles to the pan and toss to mix, being careful not to crush them. (Don't worry if they won't mix properly).

Turn the vegetables and noodles into a warmed serving bowl and top with the omelette shreds.

Chicken with a Simple Vegetable Stew

CALORIES PER SERVING: 238

Serves 2 | Preparation time: 10 minutes | Cooking time: 25 minutes

This quick and comforting dish is perfect for mid-week cooking. Celeriac is very filling and has a lovely mild flavour.

2 x 125g chicken breasts
3 tsp olive oil
zest of 1 lemon
1 rosemary sprig, leaves
    chopped
250ml hot chicken
    stock
1 shallot, sliced
½ celeriac, chopped
2 carrots, chopped
4 stems purple
    sprouting broccoli
salt and pepper

Slash the chicken breasts a couple of times. Rub 1 teaspoon of the oil all over each piece of chicken, season then rub in the lemon and rosemary. Heat a non-stick frying pan over a medium heat and fry the chicken for about 5 minutes on one side until golden.

Turn the chicken over and cook for 5 minutes on the other side. Add 100ml hot stock to the pan, cover, and continue to cook over a low heat for 15 minutes until cooked all the way through.

Meanwhile, heat the remaining teaspoon of olive oil in a pan and sauté the shallot for a minute or two until starting to turn golden. Add the celeriac and carrots, stir to mix everything together and pour in the remaining stock. Cover and simmer for 10 minutes until the celeriac is tender. Add the broccoli for the last 3 minutes of the cooking time. Season and serve, spooning the stock over the veg and the chicken juices over the chicken.

Warn Roasted Vegetable Salad

CALORIES PER SERVING: 240

Serves 4 | Preparation time: 20 minutes | Cooking time: 40 minutes

Port Salut melts beautifully and here it is tossed with warm roasted vegetables to impart a wonderfully creamy texture.

1 medium aubergine
1 medium courgette
1 small red onion
½ fennel bulb, trimmed
1 red pepper
½ tbsp chopped thyme
½ tbsp chopped sage
2 tbsp olive oil, plus a
    little extra to drizzle
½ small head of garlic
64g Port Salut cheese,
    diced
1 tbsp chopped basil
12g pitted black olives
12g pine nuts, toasted
salt and pepper
basil leaves, to garnish

for the dressing
1 tsp balsamic or sherry
    vinegar
2 tbsp extra virgin olive oil

Preheat the oven to 230°C/450°F/Mark 8. Cut the aubergines and courgettes into 2.5cm cubes. Layer in a large colander, sprinkling with a teaspoon of salt. Set aside for 30 minutes. Rinse the vegetables thoroughly to remove the salt and dry well with kitchen paper.

Cut the onion into small wedges. Remove the tough outer layer and core from the fennel, then cut into small dice. Halve, core and deseed the pepper, then cut into 2.5cm squares.

Combine all of the vegetables in a large bowl. Add the thyme, sage and oil, toss well, then transfer to a roasting tin large enough to hold the vegetables in a single layer.

Stand the half garlic head on a small sheet of foil. Drizzle over a little oil, season with salt and pepper and seal the foil to form a parcel. Sit the parcel amongst the vegetables and roast for about 40 minutes, stirring the vegetables from time to time to ensure they brown evenly. Transfer the vegetables to a large bowl and stir in the cheese.

Unwrap the garlic and scoop out the flesh into a bowl. Add the dressing ingredients, season and whisk to combine.

Pour the garlic dressing over the vegetables. Add the chopped basil, olives and pine nuts and toss lightly. Serve immediately, garnished with basil leaves.

Grilled Tomato and Mozzarella Salad

CALORIES PER SERVING: 240

Serves 4 | Preparation time: 10 minutes | Cooking time: 10 minutes

This hot salad can be prepared ahead, chilled, then grilled just before serving. Make sure you use tomatoes that are ripe and have plenty of flavour.

175g aubergine
3 tbsp olive oil
450g ripe tomatoes
150g mozzarella cheese
4 tbsp torn basil leaves
finely grated zest of
   1 lemon
1 tsp lemon juice
salt and pepper
basil leaves, to garnish

Preheat the grill to medium. Cut the aubergine into thin slices. Brush very lightly with some of the oil and place on the grill rack. Grill the aubergine slices on both sides until they are crisp and golden brown; do not let them turn too dark at this stage.

Thinly slice the tomatoes. Cut the mozzarella cheese into thin slices.

In a bowl, whisk together the remaining oil, torn basil, lemon zest and juice. Season with salt and pepper.

Arrange the tomato, aubergine and mozzarella slices, overlapping in a single layer, in a large shallow flameproof dish. Spoon the dressing evenly over the top.

Place under a hot grill for 3–4 minutes or until the mozzarella begins to melt.

Sprinkle with salt and pepper and garnish with basil leaves. Serve immediately.

Fruit and Prawn Salad with Chilli Dressing

CALORIES PER SERVING: 240

Serves 4 | Preparation time: 15 minutes | Cooking time: 2 minutes

This Indonesian salad is an unusual combination of exotic fruits and cooked prawns.
Accompanied by a hot and sour dressing, it is bursting with a whole range of exciting flavours.

1 firm ripe papaya
1 pink grapefruit
1 small firm ripe mango
1 large firm ripe banana
12 large cooked prawns
    in shells
orange zest, to garnish

for the dressing
1½ tbsp lemon juice
1 tbsp rice wine vinegar
1 tbsp caster sugar
1 tsp dark soy sauce
¼ tsp crushed red
    chillies
2 tbsp groundnut oil
pinch of salt

First make the dressing. Place the lemon juice, vinegar, sugar, soy sauce and chillies in a small saucepan and heat gently to dissolve the sugar. Remove from the heat and whisk in the oil and salt. Leave to cool.

Prepare the fruits. Peel and halve the papaya, then scoop out the seeds and thinly slice the flesh. Peel the grapefruit, removing all of the white pith, and cut out the segments between the membranes. Peel the mango, cut the flesh away from the stone, then cut into slices. Peel and slice the banana.

Arrange the fruits on a large serving platter and spoon over the dressing. Peel the prawns, leaving on the tail end shells. Arrange on top of the salad and garnish with orange zest. Serve immediately.

Herb Gnocchi with Grilled Tomato Sauce

CALORIES PER SERVING: 245

Serves 4 | Preparation time: 25 minutes | Cooking time: 30 minutes

Gnocchi are very filling so you only need to serve a small portion. Here they are served with a grilled tomato sauce, which has a lovely smoky flavour. Use a combination of red and yellow cherry tomatoes if possible, as this looks really stunning.

450g floury potatoes, peeled and halved
1 medium egg
1 tsp salt
1 tbsp finely chopped rosemary
60g plain white flour
freshly grated Parmesan cheese, to serve
rosemary sprigs, to garnish

for the sauce
450g mixed red and yellow cherry tomatoes
2 garlic cloves, sliced
1 tsp grated lemon zest
1 tbsp chopped thyme
1 tbsp chopped basil
2 tbsp olive oil
a pinch of sugar
salt and pepper

Cook the potatoes in lightly salted boiling water for 15–20 minutes until cooked; drain well and return to the pan. Set over a gentle heat to dry the potatoes out and leave to cool slightly.

Bring a large pan of water to a steady simmer. Mash the potatoes smoothly, then work in the egg, salt, rosemary and enough flour to form a soft dough. Add a little more flour if the mixture is too sticky. Transfer to a piping bag fitted with a large plain nozzle.

Meanwhile make the sauce. Preheat the grill to high. Halve the tomatoes and place in an ovenproof dish. Add the garlic, lemon zest, herbs, oil and seasoning and toss together. Sprinkle over the sugar and grill for 10 minutes until the tomatoes are charred and tender.

While the tomatoes are grilling cook the gnocchi, in batches. Pipe about six 5cm lengths directly into the boiling water, using a sharp knife to cut them off at the nozzle. Cook for 3–4 minutes, until the gnocchi float to the surface.

Remove with a slotted spoon, drain on kitchen paper and transfer to a large warmed bowl. Toss with a little olive oil and keep warm in the oven while cooking the remaining potato mixture.

Toss the cooked gnocchi with the grilled tomato sauce. Serve immediately, dusted with a little freshly grated Parmesan and garnished with rosemary.

Root Vegetable and Lentil Casserole

CALORIES PER SERVING: 260

Serves 6 | Preparation time: 20 minutes | Cooking time: 1 hour

This spicy combination of mixed root vegetables and assorted lentils makes a hearty, filling supper dish.

1 tsp cumin seeds
1 tbsp coriander seeds
1 tsp mustard seeds
25g fresh root ginger
3 tbsp olive oil
3 onions, sliced
450g carrots, chopped
350g leeks, trimmed
    and sliced
350g mooli (white
    radish), peeled and
    roughly chopped
450g button
    mushrooms, halved
2 garlic cloves, crushed
¼ tsp ground turmeric
175g split red lentils
50g brown or green
    lentils
2 tbsp chopped
    coriander leaves
salt and pepper
parsley sprigs, to
    garnish

Preheat the oven to 180°C/350°F/Mark 4. Crush the cumin, coriander and mustard seeds in a mortar with a pestle. Peel and grate or finely chop the ginger.

Heat the oil in a large flameproof casserole. Add the onions, carrots, leeks and mooli, and fry for 2–3 minutes, stirring constantly. Add the mushrooms, garlic, ginger, turmeric and crushed spices, and fry for a further 2–3 minutes, stirring.

Rinse the lentils in a colander under cold running water, then drain. Stir the lentils into the casserole with 750ml boiling water. Season with salt and pepper and return to the boil. Cover and cook in the oven for about 45 minutes or until the vegetables and lentils are tender. Stir in the coriander, and adjust the seasoning before serving, garnished with parsley.

Roast Chicken with a Devilled Sauce

CALORIES PER SERVING: 270

Serves 6 | Preparation time: 20 minutes | Cooking time: 1 hour 45 minutes

When roasts were the mainstay of British cooking, 'devilling' – using a hot sauce – was a popular way of reviving leftovers. Here, the idea is put to better use; a hot, tangy base is used for glazing a large chicken during roasting; it also forms the basis of a delicious sauce. For a more fiery sauce, add a finely chopped chilli to the devilled mixture before basting.

1 x 2.3kg chicken
1 large onion
3 garlic cloves
90ml crème fraîche
leafy herbs (e.g. basil,
   lovage or lemon
   balm), to garnish

for the devilled sauce
2 tbsp mango chutney
25g butter
2 tbsp Worcestershire
   sauce
2 tbsp grainy English
   mustard
1 tsp paprika
3 tbsp freshly squeezed
   orange juice
450g tomatoes
salt and pepper

Preheat the oven to 190°C/375°F/Mark 5. To make the devilled sauce, chop any large pieces in the chutney. Melt the butter. Mix together the butter, chutney, Worcestershire sauce, mustard, paprika, orange juice and seasoning.

Peel and chop the onion and garlic; place in the cavity of the chicken, then place the chicken in a roasting tin. Baste the skin all over with the devilled sauce. Roast in the oven, basting frequently with the sauce for 1¾ hours, or until the juices run clear when the thickest part of the thigh is pierced with a skewer. At the end of the cooking time the chicken should be slightly charred, but cover with foil towards the end of cooking if it starts to darken too much.

Meanwhile, place the tomatoes in a bowl and cover with boiling water. Leave for 30 seconds, then drain and peel the skins. Scoop out the seeds, and roughly chop the tomatoes.

Transfer the chicken to a warmed serving platter and keep warm. Skim off the fat from the juices in the roasting tin, then stir in the tomatoes and any remaining devilled sauce. Transfer the sauce to a food processor or blender and process briefly until the mixture is pulpy but retaining a little texture. Return to the pan and heat through, seasoning with salt and pepper to taste.

Meanwhile warm the crème fraîche in a small saucepan. Garnish the chicken with plenty of herbs and serve with the devilled sauce and crème fraîche.

Chicken with Herby Nut Stuffing

CALORIES PER SERVING: 307

Serves 4 | Preparation time: 15 minutes | Cooking time: 1 hour

This is a deconstructed roast chicken with stuffing. The chicken is kept lovely and juicy by being cooked in stock, while the stuffing has a satisfying crunch.

4 x 125g skinless
    chicken breasts
1 tsp dried rosemary or
    thyme
1 tsp olive oil
300ml hot chicken
    stock
salt and pepper

for the stuffing
15g butter
1 tsp olive oil
1 small onion, finely
    chopped
1 large courgette, finely
    chopped
1 celery stick, finely
    chopped
½ apple, grated
10g almonds, toasted
    and chopped
10g raisins, chopped
100g day-old
    wholemeal bread,
    whizzed into
    breadcrumbs
zest of ½ lemon
1 tsp dried rosemary or
    thyme
1 medium egg, beaten

Slash the chicken all over and season well with the dried herbs, salt and pepper and rub in the oil. Set aside.

Make the stuffing. Heat the butter and oil in a pan and add the onion, courgette and celery. Sauté over a low heat for 10–15 minutes until the onion has softened and the vegetables start to caramelize. Tip into a bowl to cool.

Once cool, add the remaining stuffing ingredients. Mix well, then spoon into a small ovenproof dish or loaf tin. Cover with foil.

Preheat the oven to 190°C/375°F/Mark 5. Line a small loaf tin or ovenproof dish with non-stick baking paper. Heat a non-stick frying pan and pan-fry the chicken for 2–3 minutes on each side until golden. Transfer to the prepared loaf tin or ovenproof dish and pour over the stock. Cover with foil.

Cook the chicken and stuffing in the oven for 45–50 minutes until the chicken is cooked through and the stuffing is golden and slightly crisp on top. Serve each chicken breast with a piece of stuffing and the stock spooned over the top.

Broad Bean and Pecorino Salad

CALORIES PER SERVING: 310

Serves 4 | Preparation time: 30 minutes | Cooking time: 1 minute

You can use frozen broad beans for this dish with good effect, but it is worth waiting until our own native broad beans are harvested to truly appreciate this salad.

450g shelled broad
  beans
4 heads of red chicory,
  trimmed
50g hard pecorino
  cheese
½ small red onion
25g hazelnuts, toasted
salt

for the dressing
2 tsp raspberry vinegar
½ tsp clear honey
4 tbsp hazelnut oil
salt and pepper

Bring a large pan of lightly salted water to a rolling boil, add the broad beans, return to the boil and cook for 1 minute. Drain and immediately refresh under cold water. Drain and pat dry. Carefully remove and discard the tough outer skins by pinching one end of the skin to release the inner bean, then place the broad beans in a large bowl.

Separate the chicory into leaves and add to the beans. Using a vegetable peeler, finely pare the cheese. Thinly slice the onion. Roughly chop the hazelnuts.

To make the dressing, place the vinegar, honey and seasoning in a small jug and gradually whisk in the oil until blended. Pour half of the dressing over the beans and chicory and toss until well coated.

Arrange the beans and chicory on individual serving plates, top with the cheese, onion and nuts and drizzle over the remaining dressing. Serve at once.

Grilled King Prawns with a Spicy Tomato and Pepper Sauce

CALORIES PER SERVING: 315

Serves 4 | Preparation time: 10 minutes | Cooking time: 40 minutes

This recipe is based on a classic Spanish romesco sauce, which can be served with almost any fish, hot or cold. Choose prawns of an equal size.

24 raw king prawns in
    shell
3 tbsp olive oil
flat-leaf parsley, to
    garnish

for the sauce
4 garlic cloves
2 ripe plum tomatoes
4 tbsp olive oil
1 onion, chopped
1 pimiento pepper in
    oil, drained and
    chopped
½ tsp dried chilli flakes
5 tbsp fish stock
2 tbsp white wine
10 blanched almonds
1 tbsp red wine vinegar
salt

To make the sauce, chop the garlic, setting aside one of the chopped cloves.

Immerse the tomatoes in a bowl of boiling water for 30 seconds, then refresh in cold water. Drain, then peel away the skins. Roughly chop the tomato flesh.

Heat 2 tablespoons of the oil in a pan, add the onion and garlic, and cook gently until softened. Add the chopped tomatoes and pimiento, together with the chilli flakes, stock and wine. Cover and simmer for 30 minutes.

Preheat the grill to medium and spread the almonds on a baking sheet. Toast the almonds under the grill until golden; alternatively dry-fry them in a pan. Transfer to a food processor or blender and grind coarsely. Add the remaining oil, the vinegar, reserved garlic and salt to taste. Work until evenly combined. Add the tomato sauce and blend until smooth.

Remove the heads from the prawns and, using a sharp knife, slit each one down the back and remove the black intestinal vein. Rinse in cold water, and dry on kitchen paper.

Preheat the grill. Toss the prawns in the oil, then spread out in the grill pan in an even layer. Grill for about 2–3 minutes on each side, until the shells have turned pink. Arrange on a serving platter, garnish with parsley and serve with the sauce.

Chicken with Tomato and Orange Sauce

315

CALORIES PER SERVING: 315

Serves 4 | Preparation time: 20 minutes | Cooking time: 35–40 minutes

These chicken breasts are filled with a light, fresh mixture of ricotta cheese, herbs and garlic, and served with a delicate sauce of fresh tomatoes simmered with a little orange.

175g ricotta cheese
4 tbsp chopped fresh
    mixed herbs (e.g.
    oregano, thyme,
    parsley and chives)
2 garlic cloves, crushed
4 x 150g skinless
    chicken breast fillets
4 slices of Parma ham
salt and pepper
leafy herbs (e.g. basil,
    lovage or lemon
    balm), to garnish
orange wedges, to
    serve

for the sauce
350g plum tomatoes
2 shallots, finely
    chopped
zest and juice of
    1 orange
1 garlic clove, crushed
1 tbsp orange
    marmalade
salt and pepper

Preheat the oven to 200°C/400°F/Mark 6. Place the ricotta cheese in a bowl and break up with a wooden spoon. Stir in the chopped herbs, garlic and seasoning.

Cut a 5cm pocket along one side of each chicken breast. Divide the filling into 4 portions and ease a portion into each pocket. Pull the chicken flesh together to encase the filling.

Wrap a slice of Parma ham around each chicken breast, lay the ham over the breast, then fold the ends under to enclose and help seal in the filling.

Place the chicken breasts in an ovenproof dish, cover with foil and cook in the oven for 35–40 minutes.

Meanwhile, make the sauce. Place the tomatoes in a large bowl, pour over enough boiling water to cover and leave for 30 seconds. Lift from the bowl and remove the skins. Roughly chop the tomato flesh.

Peel and finely chop the shallots. Put the orange zest and 2 tablespoons of the juice into a large pan. Stir in the chopped tomatoes, garlic and seasoning, cover and place over a medium heat to sweat for a few minutes. Stir in the marmalade. Bring to the boil, then simmer for about 20 minutes, until the mixture is of a spooning consistency.

Place the chicken breasts on warmed serving plates, spoon over the sauce, garnish with herbs and serve with orange wedges.

Roasted Vegetable Omelette

CALORIES PER SERVING: 320

Serves 2 | Preparation time: 5 minutes | Cooking time: 30–40 minutes

Omelettes are very versatile and can be filled with endless combinations of flavours. This is a very filling simple supper.

1 onion, peeled and cut into 6 wedges

300g peeled butternut squash, cut into bite-sized chunks

½ red pepper

2 tsp olive oil

4 broccoli florets

4 medium eggs

10g Parmesan cheese, grated

salt and pepper

Preheat the oven to 200°C/400°F/Mark 6.

Arrange the onion, squash and pepper in a roasting tin. Whisk together 1 tablespoon of cold water and 1 teaspoon of the oil and drizzle over the vegetables. Season well and toss together. Roast in the oven for 30–40 minutes until the vegetables are tender.

Blanch the broccoli in a pan of boiling water until just tender, then drain.

Preheat the grill to high. Beat the eggs in a bowl and season well. Heat the remaining olive oil in a medium non-stick frying pan. Arrange the vegetables in the pan then pour the beaten eggs over the top.

Use a wooden spoon to draw the egg away from the sides of the pan, allowing some of the uncooked egg to run into the holes. Continue to do this for a few minutes until the egg looks almost cooked. Scatter over the cheese and grill until the egg is just cooked.

Stir-fried Beef with Noodles and Chilli

CALORIES PER SERVING: 325

Serves 4 | Preparation time: 20 minutes | Cooking time: 15 minutes

For this quick noodle dish, minced beef is stir-fried with Indian curry paste, garlic, ginger and spices, then tossed with noodles and vegetables.

125g dried egg noodles

3 tbsp vegetable oil

1 tbsp dark soy sauce

1 small onion, finely chopped

2 garlic cloves, finely chopped

2.5cm piece fresh root ginger

4 Kaffir lime leaves, shredded

225g lean minced beef

2 tbsp Indian medium curry paste

1 tsp ground turmeric

½ tsp paprika

¼ tsp chilli powder

1 red pepper, deseeded and sliced

125g French beans, halved

coriander leaves, to garnish

for the sauce

2 tbsp tamarind paste

1 tbsp Thai fish sauce

2 tsp sugar

90ml beef stock

Cook the noodles according to the packet instructions, drain well and pat dry.

Meanwhile prepare the sauce. Place the tamarind paste in a bowl and whisk in the remaining ingredients until smooth. Set aside.

Heat 1 tablespoon of the oil in a wok or large frying pan, add the noodles and soy sauce and stir fry for 30 seconds. Remove from the pan and set aside.

Add the remaining oil to the pan. Add the onion and garlic, grate in the ginger and scatter over the lime leaves. Fry, stirring, for 5 minutes. Add the beef, curry paste and spices and stir-fry for 3 minutes.

Add the red pepper and beans, and stir-fry for 3 minutes. Mix in the sauce and simmer for a further 3 minutes. Carefully stir in the noodles and heat through for 2 minutes. Transfer to a warmed serving dish and garnish with the coriander.

Lamb and Bamboo Shoot Red Curry

CALORIES PER SERVING: 325

Serves 4 | Preparation time: 30 minutes | Cooking time: 45 minutes

A fiery and satisfying meaty dish. The peanuts provide a wonderful crunch, contrasting with the juicy lamb.

450g lean lamb
2 tbsp vegetable oil
1 large onion, cut into
    wedges
2 garlic cloves, finely
    chopped
2 tbsp Thai red curry
    paste
150ml lamb or beef
    stock
2 tbsp Thai fish sauce
2 tsp soft brown sugar
1 x 200g tin bamboo
    shoots, drained
1 red pepper, deseeded
2 tbsp chopped mint
1 tbsp chopped basil
25g raw peanuts,
    toasted
basil leaves, to garnish

Cut the lamb into 3cm cubes. Heat the oil in a wok or large frying pan, add the onion and garlic and fry over a medium heat for 5 minutes.

Add the lamb together with the curry paste and stir-fry for 5 minutes. Add the stock, fish sauce and sugar. Bring to the boil, lower the heat, cover and simmer gently for 20 minutes.

Meanwhile, slice the bamboo shoots and red pepper. Stir into the curry with the herbs and cook, uncovered, for a further 10 minutes. Stir in the peanuts and serve at once, garnished with basil leaves.

Turkey Melt

CALORIES PER SERVING: 332 calories

Serves 2 | Preparation time: 10 minutes | Cooking time: 10 minutes

This chunky hot sandwich won't feel like it is low-calorie at all. It's a thoroughly satisfying, speedy and very flavourful supper.

2 x 125g turkey breast
    fillets
2 tsp olive oil
1 tbsp apple chutney
20g reduced-fat
    Cheddar cheese
10g wholemeal
    breadcrumbs
2 thin slices of
    sourdough bread
2 tomatoes, sliced
50g salad leaves
1 tsp balsamic vinegar
salt and pepper

Preheat the grill to high. Season the turkey fillets. Heat 1 teaspoon of the oil in a pan and fry the turkey for 2 minutes on each side, until cooked all the way through. Spread half a tablespoon of chutney over each piece.

Transfer to a baking sheet, sprinkle with the cheese and breadcrumbs and grill until golden.

Toast the slices of sourdough. Lay slices of tomato on top of each piece, top with the turkey and serve with the salad leaves, tossed in the remaining teaspoon of oil and the balsamic vinegar.

Asparagus, Broad Bean and Parmesan Frittata 350

CALORIES PER SERVING: 350

Serves 4 | Preparation time: 35 minutes | Cooking time: 15–20 minutes

A pretty green frittata, full of fresh, clean flavours. You can use frozen broad beans for this dish – just make sure they are defrosted first.

175g small new potatoes
225g asparagus
225g shelled broad
    beans
6 medium eggs
50g freshly grated
    Parmesan cheese
3 tbsp chopped mixed
    fresh herbs (e.g. parsley,
    oregano and thyme)
45g butter
salt and pepper

Cook the potatoes in boiling salted water for 15–20 minutes until tender. Allow to cool, then slice thickly.

Meanwhile, trim the asparagus, removing any woody parts of the stems. Steam for 12 minutes until tender, then plunge into cold water to set the colour and cool completely.

Slip the broad beans out of their waxy skins. Drain the asparagus, pat dry, then cut into short lengths. Mix with the broad beans.

Put the eggs in a bowl with a good pinch of salt, plenty of pepper and half of the Parmesan. Beat thoroughly until evenly blended, then stir in the asparagus, broad beans and chopped herbs.

Melt 40g of the butter in a 25cm non-stick heavy-based frying pan. When foaming, pour in the egg mixture. Turn down the heat to as low as possible. Cook for about 15 minutes, until the frittata is set and the top is still a little runny.

Preheat the grill to medium. Scatter the cooked sliced potato over the frittata and sprinkle with the remaining Parmesan. Dot with the rest of the butter.

Place under the hot grill to brown the cheese lightly and just set the top; don't allow it to brown too much or it will dry out. Slide the frittata on to a warmed dish and cut into wedges to serve.

Chicken Breasts with Spinach and Ricotta

CALORIES PER SERVING: 360

Serves 4 | Preparation time: 30 minutes | Cooking time: 30–40 minutes

A popular recipe given a low-cal twist. The ricotta makes this an especially light but creamy option and the spinach adds a lovely flash of colour.

50g young leaf spinach
100g ricotta cheese
20g freshly grated
    Parmesan cheese
freshly grated nutmeg
4 x 150g boneless,
    skinless chicken
    breasts
4 slices smoked
    pancetta
4 rosemary sprigs
150ml dry white wine
300ml hot chicken
    stock
30g butter, chilled and
    diced
250g asparagus spears
salt and pepper

Preheat the oven to 200°C/400°F/Mark 6. Wilt the spinach in a pan and squeeze out any excess water, then roughly chop and place in a bowl. Add the ricotta, Parmesan and plenty of nutmeg, salt and pepper. Mix together well.

Using a sharp knife, make a deep horizontal slit in each chicken breast through the thicker side, to make a pocket. Spoon the filling evenly into the chicken pockets.

Wrap a slice of pancetta around each chicken breast, tucking a rosemary sprig into each. Secure with a cocktail stick, if necessary.

Lay the chicken breasts in a wide shallow pan or flameproof casserole and pour in the wine and stock. Cook in the oven for 30–40 minutes until cooked through. Remove the chicken breasts with a slotted spoon and keep warm.

Bring the liquid to the boil. Simmer rapidly until reduced by half. Remove from the heat and whisk in the cubed butter, to enrich the sauce and give it a shine. Taste and adjust the seasoning. Steam the asparagus until tender.

Serve the chicken breasts on a plate with some asparagus alongside and a little sauce spooned over the top.

Braised Monkfish Wrapped in Parma Ham with Puy Lentils

CALORIES PER SERVING: 370

Serves 6 | Preparation time: 15 minutes, plus marinating | Cooking time: 40 minutes

Monkfish is a firm-fleshed fish, which can withstand cooking methods that are more suited to meat. Here the fish is wrapped in delicate thin slices of Parma ham, pan-fried until golden, and then gently braised on a bed of Puy lentils.

1kg monkfish tail
1 small lemon
1 tbsp chopped fresh
   marjoram
6 thin slices of Parma
   ham
1 small onion
1 carrot
1 celery stick
1 garlic clove
3 tbsp olive oil
350g Puy lentils
150ml red wine
2 tomatoes, deseeded
   and diced
50g spinach
salt and pepper

Fillet the monkfish by cutting down either side of the central bone. Peel the lemon, removing all the white pith, then cut into thin slices. Lay the fish cut-side up on a board and sprinkle with the marjoram. Season with salt and pepper. Lay the lemon slices over one piece of fish, then sandwich together with the other half.

Wrap the fish in the Parma ham, making sure that it is completely covered. Tie at 5cm intervals with fine string. Cover and leave in a cool place for 1–2 hours.

Finely dice the onion, carrot and celery. Finely chop the garlic. Heat 2 tablespoons of the olive oil in a saucepan, add the garlic and vegetables and cook, stirring, for about 8 minutes, until golden. Stir in the lentils and wine and add sufficient water to cover. Bring to the boil and cook for 10 minutes.

Heat the remaining oil in a large frying pan. Add the monkfish parcel and fry, turning, until the Parma ham is browned all over. Carefully remove the fish parcel and transfer the lentils and vegetables to the frying pan. Replace the fish on top, burying it into the lentils slightly. Cover the pan and cook over a medium-low heat for 20 minutes, until the lentils are cooked and the juices from the fish run clear.

Quickly stir the tomatoes and spinach through the lentils. Serve the fish on a bed of lentils.

Paella

CALORIES PER SERVING: 405

Serves 6 | Preparation time: 30 minutes | Cooking time: 40 minutes

Paella, a traditional Spanish dish, is a typical example of the good balance of food found in the Mediterranean diet. A colourful all-in-one dish, it is excellent for an informal supper.

2 x 150g skinless
  chicken breasts
2 tbsp olive oil
225g cleaned and
  prepared squid
125g scallops
225g live mussels in
  shells
1 large onion
225g plum tomatoes
3 garlic cloves, crushed
1 tsp paprika
600ml chicken stock
1 tbsp tomato purée
350g Arborio rice
150ml dry white wine
a pinch of saffron
  threads
2 red peppers
125g shelled peas
2 tbsp chopped flat-leaf
  parsley
salt and pepper

Cut each chicken breast crosswise into 4 pieces. Heat 1 tablespoon of the oil in a paella pan, large non-stick frying pan or flameproof casserole. Toss the chicken pieces quickly in the oil to brown. Remove and set aside.

Cut off the tentacles and slice the squid into thin rings. Slice each scallop into 2 or 3 rounds, depending on their thickness. Set both aside.

Wash the mussels thoroughly in plenty of cold water, scrubbing well, and remove the beards. Discard any which do not close when tapped firmly. Place in a large pan with about 6 tablespoons of water. Bring to the boil, then cover tightly and cook for 3–4 minutes until the shells have opened; discard any that do not open. Set aside.

Finely chop the onion. Immerse the tomatoes in a bowl of boiling water for 30 seconds. Remove from the water and pull away the skins. Chop the flesh into 1cm pieces.

Heat the remaining oil in the chicken pan. Add the onion, tomatoes, garlic and paprika, and season with salt and pepper. Stir well and cook gently for 7–10 minutes, until softened.

In another pan, heat the chicken stock to just below boiling point, then stir in the tomato purée.

Cont. overleaf

Paella cont.

Add the rice to the onion and tomato mixture and cook, stirring, for 1 minute. Pour in 300ml of the hot stock and the wine. Cook, stirring, for about 7 minutes, until the liquid has been absorbed.

Meanwhile, soak the saffron threads in the remaining stock. Add to the rice with the squid, scallops and chicken. Cover and simmer gently for 15 minutes.

Meanwhile, preheat the grill to high and grill the red peppers, turning, until blackened. Cover with a damp tea towel, leave until cool enough to handle, then remove the skins. Cut the peppers in half, remove the core and seeds, then cut into thin strips.

Stir the peppers into the paella with the mussels, peas and parsley. Cook for a further 5 minutes. Check the seasoning and serve immediately.

Stir-fried King Prawns with Sesame Noodles (410)

CALORIES PER SERVING: 410

Serves 4 | Preparation time: 10 minutes | Cooking time: 10 minutes

Ginger and spring onions give piquancy to the prawns, while soy and sesame add deep flavour to the noodles and vegetables.

2 tsp sesame seeds
1 tsp salt
150g mangetout, topped and tailed
250g dried egg noodles
2 tbsp vegetable oil
16 raw king prawns
4 spring onions, roughly chopped
7.5cm piece fresh root ginger, grated
juice of 1 lime
2 tsp chopped coriander leaves
2 tbsp light soy sauce
1 tsp sesame oil
lime wedges, to serve

Put the sesame seeds in a small, heavy-based pan and shake over a medium heat until they begin to turn golden and develop a toasted aroma. Tip the toasted sesame seeds out on to a saucer.

Bring a large pan of water to the boil, add the salt and mangetout and return to the boil. Simmer for 30 seconds, then drop in the egg noodles, turn off the heat and leave to stand for 6 minutes.

Meanwhile, heat the oil in a wide frying pan. Add the prawns and cook for 1½–2 minutes on each side, scattering on the spring onions and ginger before you turn them. Squeeze on the lime juice and sprinkle on the coriander when the prawns are cooked.

Drain the noodles and mangetout and toss in the soy sauce, sesame oil and toasted sesame seeds. Transfer to a heated serving plates. Arrange the prawns and spring onions on top and serve with lime wedges.

Steak with Pepper Sauce

CALORIES PER SERVING: 413

Serves 2 | Preparation time: 10 minutes | Cooking time: 40 minutes

A simple steak supper in a rich sauce. Make sure you use beef that has been trimmed of fat.

2 medium sweet
    potatoes, chopped
2 tsp olive oil
1 garlic clove, sliced
125g mushrooms,
    quartered
2 x 150g pieces lean
    beef fillet
1 tsp roughly crushed
    black peppercorns
100g green beans
50ml red wine
150ml hot beef stock
1 tsp redcurrant jelly
1 tsp butter
50g watercress
salt and pepper

Put the sweet potatoes in a pan and cover with cold water. Bring to the boil and simmer for around 15 minutes, until tender. Drain well, then season and mash.

Heat 1 teaspoon of the oil in a pan and add the garlic. Cook for 1 minute. Add the mushrooms, season, and cover the pan with a lid. Cook for 3–4 minutes, shaking the pan every now and then.

Rub 1 teaspoon of the oil over each piece of beef and press in the crushed peppercorns.

Heat a non-stick frying pan and cook the beef for 3–5 minutes on each side for medium done. Set aside on a warm plate, cover with foil and rest. Steam the green beans.

Add the red wine, stock and jelly to the frying pan and season. Bring to the boil and simmer for a few minutes until syrupy. Whisk in the butter.

Divide the mash and green beans between two plates. Place the beef on top, then spoon over the mushrooms and sauce, and serve with a handful of watercress.

Fettucine with Gorgonzola and Spinach

CALORIES PER SERVING: 420

Serves 6 | Preparation time: 15 minutes | Cooking time: 10 minutes

The rich and creamy flavour of this pasta sauce belies its few simple ingredients. Use small young, tender spinach leaves if possible.

350g young leaf
    spinach
225g Gorgonzola
    cheese
75ml semi-skimmed
    milk
25g butter
400g fresh fettucine,
    tagliatelle or long
    fusilli
salt and pepper
freshly grated nutmeg,
    to serve

Wash the spinach thoroughly and remove any large stalks. Place in a clean saucepan and cook, stirring, over a medium high heat for 2–3 minutes until wilted. There is no need to add extra water – the small amount clinging to the leaves after washing provides sufficient moisture. Drain well in a colander or sieve, pressing out any excess liquid.

Cut the Gorgonzola into small pieces. Place in a clean pan with the milk and butter. Heat gently, stirring, until melted to a creamy sauce. Stir in the drained spinach. Season to taste with pepper; salt may not be necessary because the Gorgonzola is quite salty.

Just before serving, cook the pasta in a large pan of boiling salted water according to packet instructions.

Drain the pasta thoroughly and add to the sauce. Toss well to mix. Serve at once, sprinkled with a little freshly grated nutmeg.

Grilled Chicken with a Spiced Yoghurt Crust

CALORIES PER SERVING: 440

Serves 4 │ Preparation time: 10 minutes, plus marinating │ Cooking time: 20 minutes

Yoghurt makes a wonderful basis for a marinade, as it tenderizes and flavours yet doesn't disappear during cooking. Instead it forms a delicious soft crust which protects the meat from the fierce heat of the grill.

4 x 125g skinless
    chicken breasts
1 tbsp coriander seeds
1 tsp ground cumin
2 tsp mild curry paste
1 garlic clove, crushed
450ml Greek-style
    yoghurt
3 tbsp chopped
    coriander
200g quick-cook brown
    rice
200g spinach leaves
¼ red onion, finely
    sliced
salt and pepper
1 lemon, cut into
    wedges, to serve

Slash the chicken breasts two or three times. Crush the coriander seeds, using a pestle and mortar. Mix with the cumin, curry paste, garlic and yoghurt in a large shallow dish. Season with salt and pepper and stir in the fresh coriander.

Add the chicken and turn to coat thoroughly with the spiced yoghurt mixture. Leave to marinate for 30 minutes, or cover and place in the fridge overnight.

Preheat the grill to high. Grill the chicken, turning occasionally, for about 20 minutes or until cooked through.

Cook the rice according to the packet instructions. Wash the spinach and cook in a hot pan until just wilted. Toss the rice with the spinach and red onion.

Serve the chicken with the rice and a wedge of lemon to squeeze over.

snacks and drinks

Koftas

CALORIES PER KOFTA: 40

Makes 24 | Preparation time: 20 minutes | Cooking time: 10 minutes

These make a fantastic snack and can be made well in advance, frozen and reheated straight from the freezer.

1 small onion, quartered
1 garlic clove, peeled
2.5cm piece fresh root
    ginger, halved
1 tsp ground cumin
1 tsp ground coriander
3 tbsp ghee or
    vegetable oil
450g minced beef
3 tbsp chopped
    coriander
1 medium egg
salt and pepper

Put the onion, garlic and ginger in a blender or food processor and work until finely chopped. Add the spices and process until evenly mixed.

Heat 1 tablespoon of the ghee or oil in a frying pan and add the onion paste. Cook over a medium heat for 2–3 minutes, stirring all the time. Remove from the heat and allow to cool.

Put the minced beef in a bowl and break it up with a fork. Add the chopped coriander and season with salt and pepper. Add the cooled onion paste and mix thoroughly until evenly incorporated. Add just sufficient beaten egg to bind; don't add too much or the mixture will be too sticky to shape.

Using lightly floured hands, shape the spiced beef mixture into 24 small balls.

Heat the remaining ghee or oil in the frying pan and add the koftas (see note). Cook for about 5 minutes or until browned on all sides and cooked right through, shaking the pan as they cook to ensure they brown evenly. Drain the koftas on kitchen paper and serve hot.

Note: If your frying pan is small you may need to cook the koftas in a couple of batches.

Spice Finger Biscuits

CALORIES PER BISCUIT: 50

Makes 18 | Preparation time: 12 minutes | Cooking time: 15 minutes

Crisp and light with a slightly chewy centre, these simple finger biscuits have an almost meringue-like texture. The deliciously spicy after-taste is accentuated by the sprinkling of black pepper, although this can be omitted for a more conventional biscuit. These biscuits cannot be frozen but if stored in an airtight jar will last for up to a week.

1 medium egg white
2 tsp cornflour
½ tsp ground cinnamon
½ tsp ground ginger
125g caster sugar
75g ground almonds
black pepper and extra
    spice, for sprinkling

Preheat the oven to 180°C/350°F/Mark 4. Line a large baking sheet with non-stick baking paper.

Whisk the egg white in a bowl until stiff, but not dry. Sift in the cornflour and spices. Add the sugar and ground almonds and gently stir the ingredients together to form a light sticky paste.

Place the mixture in a large piping bag, fitted with a 1cm plain nozzle. Pipe 7cm finger lengths on to the baking sheet, spacing them slightly apart. Sprinkle with pepper and a little extra spice and bake for 12 minutes or until crisp and golden. Transfer to a wire rack to cool.

Note: If you don't have a suitable piping nozzle, spoon the mixture onto the lined baking sheet instead.

Tropical Smoothie

CALORIES PER SERVING: 76

Serves 1 | Preparation time: 5 minutes

This effortlessly easy smoothie will give you a boost at any time of day. The cinnamon gives it an extra layer of flavour, which contrasts with the sweetness of the mango. Try it with other fruits for endless combinations.

½ mango, peeled and
    stoned
1 apple, unpeeled
juice of ½ lime
a pinch of cinnamon

Roughly chop the fruit and put it in a blender with the lime juice, cinnamon and 50ml water.

Whiz until smooth, then pour into a glass and enjoy!

Citrus Poached Pears

CALORIES PER SERVING: 90

Serves 4 | Preparation time: 5 minutes | Cooking time: 40 minutes

The star anise in this light, fruity snack provides an exotic flavour and enhances the sweetness of the pears and honey. This dish can double up as a refreshing pudding.

4 pears, peeled
zest and juice of 2
    oranges and 1 lemon
2 tsp clear honey
1 cinnamon stick
1 star anise

Place the pears in a pan with the orange juice, lemon, honey, cinnamon and star anise. Add 200ml water and cover with a circle of greaseproof paper. Put the lid on the pan and bring to the boil then turn down the heat and simmer for 20–30 minutes, until the pears are tender.

Remove the pears from the liquid and set aside. Bring the mixture to the boil and simmer for a few minutes to reduce to about 100ml. Serve each pear with the juice drizzled over.

Biscotti

CALORIES PER BISCUIT: 90

Makes 50 | Preparation time: 25 minutes | Cooking time: 45 minutes

These light, crunchy biscuits, studded with toasted almonds and with a hint of orange are irresistible. They will keep in an airtight jar for a couple of weeks.

175g whole blanched almonds
1 tbsp coriander seeds
125g unsalted butter, softened
200g granulated sugar
2 medium eggs, beaten
finely grated zest of 1 orange
1 tbsp Grand Marnier or other orange liqueur
1½ tsp baking powder
½ tsp salt
350g plain white flour
75g coarse-grain polenta (ordinary or quick-cook)

Preheat the oven to 170°C/325°F/Mark 3. Spread the almonds on a baking sheet and toast in the oven for 5–10 minutes until golden. Allow to cool. Coarsely chop one third of the toasted nuts and mix with the whole ones. Lightly crush the coriander seeds.

In a bowl, cream the butter with the sugar until just mixed. Beat in the eggs, orange zest, liqueur, baking powder and salt. Stir in 275g of the flour, the polenta, almonds and crushed coriander

Turn the dough on to a floured work surface and knead until smooth, adding the remaining flour little by little, until the dough is soft but not sticky. It may not be necessary to add all of the flour.

Divide the dough into four equal pieces and roll each into a 5cm wide, 2cm deep sausage. Place these on 2 greased baking sheets and bake for about 35 minutes, until just golden around the edges.

Carefully transfer to a wire rack. Allow to cool for 10 minutes, then cut diagonally into 1-cm thick slices. Place these slices, cut-side down, on the baking sheets and bake for another 10 minutes until golden brown. Transfer to a wire rack to cool completely.

Note: Polenta is maize meal and can be bought in different grades. Use coarse meal for biscotti.

Crispbread Toppings

Serves 1

Each of these delicious toppings can be spread liberally on a crispbread. The individual calorie counts include the crispbreads. Alternatively, use them as dips for crunchy veg, like carrots and celery.

Spicy avocado

CALORIES PER SERVING: 100
Preparation time: 5 minutes

Mash a quarter of an avocado with a squeeze of lime and a pinch of chilli flakes. Season well with salt and pepper, then spoon on to a crispbread and top with sliced tomato.

Herb and mustard spread

CALORIES PER SERVING: 75
Preparation time: 5 minutes

Put 20g low-fat cream cheese in a bowl and beat in 1 teaspoon of grainy mustard and 1 tablespoon of freshly chopped herbs (a mixture of parsley, chives and thyme is ideal) and a squeeze of lemon. Season and mix again then spoon on to the crispbread.

Butterbean hummus

CALORIES PER SERVING: 98
Preparation time: 3 minutes

Drain a 400g can of butterbeans and blitz in a blender with the juice of 1 lemon and 1 teaspoon each of ground cumin and coriander seeds. Season well with salt and pepper and top 2 crispbreads with 2 tablespoons of hummus each, and sprinkle with paprika. Keep the rest of the hummus in the fridge, covered; it will last for a couple of days.

Hot and Sour Soup

CALORIES PER SERVING: 100

Serves 2 | Preparation time: 15 minutes | Cooking time: 25 minutes

Look out for packs of Thai mixed spices in larger supermarkets. Each pack usually contains a piece of lemon grass, some Kaffir lime leaves, a couple of hot chillies and a few pieces of kuchai (garlic chives). If you are unable to find a ready-made pack, buy each of these ingredients separately.

1 x packet of fresh Thai mixed spices (see above)

2 garlic cloves, finely sliced

2.5cm piece fresh root ginger, finely sliced

a handful of coriander

1.2 litres chicken stock

1 x 150g skinless chicken breast fillet

125g mushrooms, preferably shiitake or baby button mushrooms

1–2 spring onions, to garnish

juice of 2 limes

2 tbsp light soy sauce

Prepare the herbs by crushing the lemon grass using a rolling pin. Finely slice the chillies (retaining the seeds). Put the Thai herbs in a large saucepan along with the garlic, ginger, half the coriander and the stock. Cover and bring to the boil.

Meanwhile, cut the chicken into strips and halve or slice any larger mushrooms. When the stock has come to the boil, reduce the heat so that it is just simmering. Drop the chicken and mushrooms into the soup. Cover and simmer gently for 20 minutes.

Meanwhile, trim the spring onions and cut into 7.5cm lengths. Halve each piece lengthways, then cut into very fine shreds. Drop them into a bowl of cold water and leave in the refrigerator to curl. (If you're short of time you could simply trim the spring onions and cut into thin slices on the diagonal).

Check that the chicken is cooked. Add the lime juice and soy sauce to the soup, then taste. The flavour should be fairly hot and faintly sour. If it needs more salt, add a little extra soy sauce. Remove and discard the coriander.

Drain the curled spring onion shreds. Ladle the soup into warmed individual bowls and top each with a pile of onion shreds and the rest of the fresh coriander.

Saffron Scones

CALORIES PER SERVING: 110

Makes 12 | Preparation time: 15 minutes, plus infusing time | Cooking time: 10 minutes

With its golden colour, wonderful aroma and intriguing taste, regal saffron gives an exciting lift to the humble scone. These scones can be frozen.

1 tsp saffron threads
150ml milk
225g self-raising white
    flour
a pinch of salt
1 tsp baking powder
40g unsalted butter or
    margarine
2 tbsp caster sugar
1 medium egg, beaten,
    to glaze

Preheat the oven to 220°C/425°F/Mark 7. Lightly grease a baking sheet.

Roughly break up the saffron threads and place in a saucepan with half of the milk. Bring just to the boil, then remove from the heat and leave to infuse for 20 minutes.

Sift the flour, salt and baking powder into a bowl. Add the butter, cut into small pieces, and rub in using your fingertips, until the mixture resembles fine breadcrumbs. Stir in the sugar.

Stir in the saffron milk and half of the remaining milk. Mix with a round-bladed knife to a soft dough, adding the rest of the milk if the mixture is too dry; it should be soft and slightly sticky.

Knead lightly and roll out to a 2cm thickness. Cut out rounds, using a 5cm cutter. Place on the baking sheet and brush the tops with the beaten egg. Bake for 10–12 minutes until well risen and golden brown. Transfer to a wire rack to cool.

Oaty Fruit Bites

CALORIES PER BITE: 113

Makes 16 │ Preparation time: 10 minutes │ Cooking time: 20 minutes

The oats will provide slow-release energy to help keep you full. These freeze really well so wrap up any that you aren't going to eat in cling film and freeze them for up to a month.

75g clear honey

2 medium eggs

125g self-raising
   wholemeal flour

75g oats

75g sultanas

20g flaked almonds

50g butter, melted

75ml milk

1 tsp mixed spice

zest of 1 orange

Preheat the oven to 200˚C/400˚F/Mark 6. Line a shallow 17cm-square baking tin with non-stick baking paper.

Beat the honey and eggs together in a bowl. Sift in the flour, then add the rest of the ingredients and fold together with a large metal spoon. Spoon into the prepared tin, spread out evenly and bake for 20 minutes.

Using the edges of the baking parchment, lift out the bake and transfer to a wire rack. Leave to cool then cut into 16 squares.

Rich and Dark Spiced Hot Chocolate

CALORIES PER SERVING: 114

Serves 1 | Preparation time: 2 minutes | Cooking time: 5 minutes

Sometimes only chocolate is the answer. This lightly spiced chocolate drink is rich and indulgent and miraculously low in calories.

100ml semi-skimmed milk
50ml water
10g dark chocolate (70 per cent cocoa solids), grated
1 tsp cocoa powder
½ tsp sugar
1 star anise
a good pinch of mixed spice
¼ vanilla pod

Pour the milk and water into a pan and add the chocolate, cocoa powder, sugar, star anise and mixed spice. Split the piece of vanilla pod lengthways and scrape the seeds into the liquid. Add the pod, too.

Place the pan over a medium heat and bring to the boil, whisking all the time to dissolve the chocolate in the liquid. As soon as the mixture is boiling, strain into a cup and serve.

Green Apple Sorbet

CALORIES PER SERVING: 118

Serves 4 │ Preparation time: 25 minutes, plus chilling and freezing time │
Cooking time: 10 minutes

Make this fresh, summery sorbet with sweet but sharp Granny Smith apples – taste
one to make sure they're sharp enough. The Calvados provides an extra richness,
but feel free to leave it out if you prefer.

450g Granny Smith
   apples
50g caster sugar
2 tbsp lemon or lime
   juice
3 tbsp Calvados
1 medium egg white,
   lightly beaten

Peel, halve and core the apples. Place in a saucepan with the sugar and lemon or lime juice. Cover and simmer for 5–10 minutes until tender.

Purée the soft apple mixture in a blender or food processor, then sieve to remove any lumps. Cool, chill, then stir in the Calvados. Churn in an ice-cream maker according to the manufacturer's instructions, adding the beaten egg white halfway through freezing. If you do not have an ice-cream maker, transfer to a shallow container and freeze for 2 hours. Remove from the freezer and beat well to break down any ice crystals that may have formed. Return to the freezer for a further 1 hour, then beat again. Repeat once more. Freeze for several hours, and just before the sorbet is almost firm, stir in the egg white. Freeze again until required.

Fruit Salad

CALORIES PER SERVING: 125

Serves 6 | Preparation time: 20 minutes, plus infusing and chilling time |
Cooking time: 5 minutes

This refreshing fruit salad is enhanced with a cardamom and mint syrup. Choose ripe
fruit in optimum condition. Pineapples should have a rich golden brown skin and a sweet
aroma; mangoes should give slightly when gently pressed.

50g caster sugar
4 green cardamom
    pods
6 large mint sprigs
finely grated zest and
    juice of 1 lime
1 medium pineapple
1 large mango
3 small juicy oranges
1 medium papaya

Put the sugar in a small heavy-based pan with 200ml
water. Crush the cardamom with a rolling pin to split the
pods slightly. Crush 4 mint sprigs in the same way. Add the
crushed mint and cardamom to the pan.

Heat the mixture gently until the sugar dissolves, then bring
to the boil and boil for 1 minute. Allow to cool and infuse
for at least 1 hour or until completely cold. Discard the mint
sprigs and cardamom pods.

Strip the leaves from the remaining mint sprigs and add
them to the sugar syrup with the lime zest and juice. Pour
into a bowl and chill while preparing the fruit.

Peel the pineapple, halve and discard the tough central core.
Cut the flesh into large chunks. Cut the mango across either
side of the stone, then cut the flesh into large slices and peel
off the skin. Chop the flesh surrounding the stone. Peel the
oranges, then cut each one into wedges. Cut the papaya in
half and scoop out the seeds with a teaspoon. Cut the flesh
into slices and remove the skin.

Arrange the fruit in a shallow serving dish and pour over
the syrup. Cover the bowl and chill in the refrigerator for
30 minutes before serving.

Note: Don't cut the fruit up too small; keep the pieces
chunky and attractive.

Mango, Ginger and Citrus Sorbet

CALORIES PER SERVING: 130

Serves 4 | Preparation time: 25 minutes, plus freezing time | Cooking time: 4 minutes

Mangoes are ideal for making sorbets as their creamy texture lends itself perfectly to the freezing process. The sweetness of the ginger and mango is balanced by the lime juice to produce a tangy, refreshing snack.

2 x 400g mangoes
25g preserved stem
    ginger, drained
50ml syrup from the
    stem ginger jar
40g caster sugar
finely grated zest and
    juice of 3 limes

Peel the mangoes, using a potato peeler, then cut down either side of the central stone; cut away as much of the remaining flesh as possible. Chop the mango flesh and purée in a blender or food processor until very smooth. Transfer to a bowl and set aside. Finely chop the stem ginger and stir into the purée.

Place the ginger syrup in a small pan with the sugar, lime zest and juice, and add 90ml water. Heat gently, stirring until the sugar has dissolved. Bring to the boil and simmer for 3 minutes. Remove from the heat and leave to cool.

Strain the cooled syrup through a fine sieve into the puréed mango mixture and stir well. Transfer to a plastic container and freeze for 2 hours.

Remove from the freezer and beat well to break down any ice crystals that may have formed. Return to the freezer for a further 1 hour, then beat again. Repeat once more. Freeze for several hours until firm, or until required. Transfer the sorbet to the refrigerator about 20 minutes before serving to soften slightly. Scoop into individual glass dishes to serve.

Almond Fudge Crumbles

CALORIES PER BISCUIT: 130

Makes 20 | Preparation time: 10 minutes | Cooking time: 12 minutes

At times the only answer is a nibble of something sweet. Hidden pieces of crushed almond flakes and chewy fudge marry perfectly in these simple biscuits. This recipe makes enough dough for 20 biscuits, so use half and then freeze the other half for up to a month.

200g plain white flour
a pinch of salt
½ tsp bicarbonate of
    soda
125g unsalted butter
125g muscovado sugar
1 medium egg
1 tsp almond essence
75g flaked almonds,
    crumbled
50g vanilla fudge, finely
    diced
icing sugar, for dusting

Preheat the oven to 190°C/375°F/Mark 5. Lightly grease two baking sheets.

Sift the flour, salt and bicarbonate of soda into a bowl. Add the butter, cut into small pieces, and rub in using your fingertips.

Add the sugar, egg, almond essence, 65g of the flaked almonds and 40g of the fudge and mix to form a fairly firm dough.

Turn on to a lightly floured surface and roll into a cylinder about 23cm long. (At this point you can freeze any of the dough you're not planning on using.) Cut the dough into rounds and arrange them on the prepared baking sheets leaving a little space between each one.

Scatter over the remaining almonds and fudge and press down lightly. Bake the biscuits for 12 minutes, until turning golden around the edges. Leave on the baking sheets for 5 minutes, then transfer to a wire rack to cool. Serve dusted with icing sugar.

Spicy Trail Mix

CALORIES PER SERVING: 154

Makes 10 x 30g servings | Preparation time: 5 minutes | Cooking time: 15 minutes

Crunchy and spicy, this nutty mix will stave off mid-afternoon hunger pangs. Keep a portion in your bag for when you're out and about and store the rest in an airtight jar, where it will keep for about a week.

50g pistachio nuts
50g Brazil nuts
50g almonds
50g cashew nuts
1 tsp olive oil
½ tsp garlic granules
1 tsp cayenne pepper
1 tsp chopped rosemary
    leaves
50g sultanas
50g dried cranberries

Preheat the oven to 200°C/400°F/Mark 6. Put the nuts in a roasting tin and drizzle over the oil. Add the garlic, cayenne and rosemary and mix everything together. Make sure the nuts are coated in the oil.

Roast in the oven for 10 minutes then add the sultanas and cranberries and continue to roast for a further 5 minutes.

Remove from the oven and leave to cool slightly. Store in an airtight jar for up to a week.

Individual Summer Puddings

CALORIES PER SERVING: 160

Serves 6 | Preparation time: 30 minutes, plus chilling time | Cooking time: 12 minutes

An old favourite, individual summer puddings are ideal to serve as part of a healthy diet, especially if you use wholemeal bread. Fruit of any description is good to use here – summer puddings can be made into autumn puddings by using apples, pears and plums.

12 large slices of
    wholemeal bread,
    crusts removed
300g blackberries
400g raspberries
125g gooseberries
175g redcurrants
150ml red grape juice
2 tbsp chopped mint
artificial sweetener,
    to taste

Line six 150ml-dariole moulds or individual pudding basins with cling film. Cut a 5cm circle of bread to fit the base of each mould. Cut six 7.5cm circles of bread and set aside. Cut the remaining bread into strips and use to line the sides of the moulds completely.

Hull the blackberries and raspberries, and top and tail the gooseberries. Strip the redcurrants off their stalks.

Place the gooseberries in a saucepan with the grape juice, cover and cook for 5 minutes. Add the remaining fruit and cook gently until the currants start to burst and the juice runs; this will take 5–7 minutes. Stir the mint into the fruit and add sweetener, to taste.

While the fruit is still warm, spoon into the lined moulds, using a slotted spoon, and pour on sufficient fruit juice to moisten. Reserve the rest of the fruit juice. Cover with the reserved bread rounds. Top each mould with a saucer or plate and press down with a heavy weight. Place in the fridge for several hours or overnight.

Turn out the puddings on to serving plates and pour on the reserved juice to cover them.

Spiced Baked Apple

CALORIES PER SERVING: 163

Serves 1 | Preparation time: 10 minutes | Cooking time: 45–50 minutes

A sweet and filling snack that you could even serve as a pudding. You could use another type of apple, but Bramleys are ideal because they hold their shape as they cook.

1 Bramley apple
1 ready-to-eat dried
    apricot, finely
    chopped
1 ready-to-eat dried
    date, finely chopped
4 whole almonds, finely
    chopped
½ tsp mixed spice
½ tsp clear honey
juice of ½ orange
1 slightly heaped tbsp
    fat-free Greek-style
    yoghurt

Preheat the oven to 200°C/400°F/Mark 6.

Core the apple and use a sharp knife to cut the skin round the equator – this stops the apple from exploding during baking.

Mix together the chopped apricot, date, almonds, mixed spice, honey and orange juice.

Place the apple in a small ovenproof dish and spoon the fruit mixture into the cavity of the apple. Pour enough boiling water into the dish to just cover the base, then cover the whole dish with foil. Bake for 45–50 minutes, until the apple is soft. Serve with the yoghurt.

Egg 'Mayo' on Rye

CALORIES PER SERVING: 190

Serves 1 | Preparation time: 10 minutes | Cooking time: 10 minutes

Eggs are powerhouses of nutrition and will keep you feeling full for hours. Try this light mayo-style dressing and serve on a slice of dark rye bread. The pea shoots will provide a satisfying, fresh crunch.

1 medium egg
1 tsp olive oil
1 tsp Dijon mustard
a squeeze of lemon
    juice
1 tbsp chopped cress
½ slice dark rye bread
    (30g)
salt and pepper
a handful of watercress
    or pea shoots, to
    serve

Place the egg in a pan of water and bring to the boil. Simmer for 7 minutes. Lift the cooked egg out of the pan and hold under cold running water to cool quickly.

Remove the shell from the egg. Using a fork, roughly crush the egg in a bowl.

Whisk together the oil, mustard and lemon juice and season well. Add to the egg along with some chopped cress and fold everything together.

Spoon on top of the rye bread and top with the watercress or pea shoots.

Pickled Salmon on Rye

CALORIES PER SERVING: 199

Serves 2 | Preparation time: 25 minutes, plus resting and chilling time

This homemade gravadlax incorporates a dash of teriyaki marinade and a little fresh ginger to give it a Japanese overtone. Slice it vertically and very finely and serve on dark rye bread. The pickled salmon keeps well in the fridge.

125g salmon, filleted and trimmed, but not skinned
¼ tsp vegetable oil
0.5cm piece fresh root ginger
1 tsp sugar
1 tsp coarse sea salt
1 tsp white peppercorns, crushed
½ tbsp vodka or rice wine (saki)
1 tsp teriyaki marinade
2 thin slices of dark rye bread
50g salad leaves
½ tsp chopped chives, to garnish

for the sauce
1 tbsp horseradish sauce (or milder creamed horseradish)
0.5cm piece fresh root ginger

Remove any small bones from the salmon with tweezers. Rub the flesh with the oil. Peel and finely chop the ginger and mix with the sugar, salt and crushed peppercorns.

Put the salmon fillet, skin-side down, on a large sheet of greaseproof paper on top of a sheet of kitchen foil. Spread the spice mixture evenly over the flesh. Moisten with the vodka and teriyaki marinade. Wrap up tightly in the paper and then the foil. Place in a non-corrosive dish and cover with a small plate. Place a 450g weight on top and leave at cool room temperature for 4 hours.

After 4 hours, turn the parcel over and replace the plate and weight. Leave for a further 4 hours, then remove the weight and refrigerate for 4 hours. The salmon is ready to eat, but the longer it sits in the marinade, the stronger the flavour will become.

For the sauce, put the horseradish in a small bowl. Peel and chop the ginger and squeeze through a garlic press into the horseradish, and mix to combine.

Unwrap the salmon parcel, retaining the juices, and scrape off the excess peppercorns. Slice the salmon vertically, into 0.5cm-thick slices, then cut horizontally, close to the skin, to release each slice.

Spread a little sauce on each slice of rye bread. Arrange the pickled salmon slices on the bread. Serve with a little salad, a drizzle of marinade and a sprinkling of chives.

Spiced Pork Balls with Sweet Chilli Sauce

CALORIES PER SERVING: 200 (39 calories per pork ball)

Makes 20 balls | Preparation time: 10 minutes | Cooking time: 10 minutes

These hearty little meaty snacks are deliciously spicy, and don't seem like a low-calorie option at all. Served with the chilli sauce dip and a crisp salad, they make a very satisfying snack, or could even be served as a light lunch or dinner.

2.5cm piece fresh root ginger, peeled and halved

2 garlic cloves, peeled

2 shallots, peeled and quartered

2 red chillies

1 tsp Chinese five spice

6 tbsp chopped coriander

500g pork fillet, roughly chopped

1 medium egg, beaten

a little plain flour, for rolling

2 tsp vegetable oil

12 Little Gem lettuce leaves

salt and white pepper

4 spring onions, shredded, to garnish

for the sauce

2 tbsp sweet chilli sauce

1 tbsp rice wine vinegar

½ small carrot, coarsely grated

⅛ cucumber, grated

Place the ginger, garlic, shallots and chillies (remove the seeds if you don't like it too hot) in a food processor or blender and blitz until finely chopped.

Add the five spice, coriander, pork and egg. Process again until evenly mixed. Season with the salt and white pepper.

Using lightly floured hands, shape the mixture into 20 walnut-sized balls.

Heat a little oil in a non-stick frying pan and fry the balls, in batches, on each side until golden and cooked through.

In a small bowl, stir together the sweet chilli sauce, vinegar, carrot and cucumber. Divide the Little Gem lettuce leaves between four plates, top with the balls, drizzle with the sauce and serve garnished with shredded spring onions.

meal plans

Day 1

TOTAL CALORIES PER SERVING: 481

136   **Breakfast:** Mini Pancakes with Smoked Salmon   (page 16)

105   **Lunch:** Sugar Snap Peas with a Minted Lemon Dip   (page 42)

240   **Dinner:** Warm Roasted Vegetable Salad   (page 121)

Day 2

TOTAL CALORIES PER SERVING: 497

204 **Breakfast:** Huevos Rancheros (page 22)

98 **Snack:** Butterbean Hummus Crispbread (page 157)

195 **Dinner:** Tomato and Peach Salad with Avocado Salsa (page 111)

Day 3

TOTAL CALORIES PER SERVING: 508

(112) **Breakfast:** Melon with Summer Fruits (page 13)

(171) **Lunch:** Prawn and Rice Noodle Salad (page 49)

(135) **Dinner:** Grilled Stuffed Peppers (page 98)

(90) **Snack:** Biscotti (page 155)

Day 4

TOTAL CALORIES PER SERVING: 518

249   **Breakfast:** Eggs with Smoked Salmon   (page 29)

229   **Lunch:** Asian-style Chicken Noodle Soup   (page 60)

40   **Snack:** Koftas   (page 152)

Day 5

 528

TOTAL CALORIES PER SERVING: 528

 228   **Breakfast:** Parma Ham, Melon and Ricotta Salad (page 26)

100   **Lunch:** Mushroom Pâté with Madeira (page 40)

200   **Dinner:** Chinese Beef (page 114)

Day 6

TOTAL CALORIES PER SERVING: 538

105 **Breakfast:** Chilled Melon and Ginger Salad (page 12)

215 **Lunch:** Indian Spiced Fritters with Coriander Chutney (page 59)

100 **Dinner:** Thai Fishcakes (page 96)

118 **Snack:** Green Apple Sorbet (page 164)

Day 7

TOTAL CALORIES PER SERVING: 555

76 **Snack:** Tropical Smoothie (page 154)

180 **Lunch:** Fattoush (page 53)

185 **Dinner:** Butternut Squash Soup with Parmesan Crostini (page 108)

114 **Snack:** Rich and Dark Spiced Hot Chocolate (page 163)

Day 8

TOTAL CALORIES PER SERVING: 570

 Breakfast: Savoury Muffins (page 25)

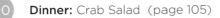 **Lunch:** Fennel and Orange Salad (page 54)

Dinner: Crab Salad (page 105)

index